CREDIT REPAIR:

RAISING YOUR CREDIT SCORE TO 720+

TABLE OF CONTENTS

Introduction

Chapter One Fundamentals of Credit Repair

Chapter Two Utilizing Your Credit Score: Good or Bad

Chapter Three Managing Your Debts and Credit

Chapter Four Understanding Bankruptcy, Judgment and Liens

Chapter Five Dealing with Foreclosure

Chapter Six The Truths about Credit Bureaus

Chapter Seven Disputing Negative Accounts and Errors

Chapter Eight Trusted Techniques for Repairing Your Credit

Conclusion Final DIY Ideas and Tips to Bear in Mind as you Repair your Credit

Copyright 2019 by Ruben Hanson

All rights reserved. This book or parts thereof may not be reproduced in any form, stored in any retrieval system, or transmitted in any form by any means—electronic, mechanical, photocopy, recording, or otherwise—without prior written permission of the publisher, except as provided by United States of America copyright law.

All rights reserved. No portion of this book may be reproduced in any form without permission from the publisher, except as permitted by U.S. copyright law.

Introduction

Credit and credit repair are key terms in the modern world that every individual hoping to establish a steady financial life for themselves must understand. If you are reading this book, you are most definitely interested in repairing your credit or hoping to learn how to build a good credit score for yourself. I cannot explain in simple words what the value of a good credit score to a person's business and personal financial life is. Most people learn this lesson the hard way after having suffered one rejection or the other at the point of securing a loan, renting a coveted apartment, or after having been slammed with very high interests by a mortgage firm. If you have learned your lesson the hard way, it is not too late to make amends and repair your credit from a low credit score to a high credit score. However, before we go into all the details on how you can fix your credit, let us delve briefly into the concepts of credit and credit repair just in case they are entirely new to you.

What is Credit?

To put it most simply at this introductory phase, I will adopt the Wikipedia Dictionary meaning of credit thus: *Credit is the trust which allows one party to provide money or resources to another party wherein the second party does not reimburse the first party immediately but promises either to repay or return those resources at a later date.* Put differently, this is the confidence your prospective employer has in you to commit serious monetary transactions into your charge; the assurance your landlord or landlady has that you will be able to meet up with your rent after the first payment; the confidence a financial firm has that you are capable of repaying your loans as and when due, and several other finance-related situations. This assurance or confidence is measured in figures known as credit score. On the overall, your credit score ranges from 300 to 850 even though there are various classifications. Notwithstanding, a common agreement is that a credit score below 450 is considered very bad; within the range of 450 and 650 is considered bad; within the range of 650 and 700 is fair; 700 and 750 is good, and a score above 750 is considered an excellent one. In some other classifications, however, 720 is considered the benchmark for an excellent credit score. Credit bureaus such as Equifax, TransUnion, and Experian are major organizations that can present you with your annual credit reports. To repair your credit, the right place to start is to check your present credit report and see what information is responsible for the low score. There are also several online platforms where you can check your credit score for free. Your credit score is generated using your credit history and financial involvement. All these make up the information that comprises your credit reports. Staying updated with your credit report keeps you in the know of the situation of your credit, and what areas to focus on to help you boost it.

A number of factors influences your credit score including your history of payment of bills, absence of credit blunders, among others. Loan firms, employers, and other financial firms consider your credit score before giving out loans or other opportunities. Your credit score also influences the rate of interest you are charged on your loans. A low credit score will deprive you of many golden privileges that could have otherwise bettered your life. This explains why you need to repair your credit and get it soaring from a low score to a high one.

What is Credit Repair?

Credit repair describes the entire process of fixing a troubled credit, the result of which is a higher credit score. This might include removing negative information, disputing inaccurate information on your credit report, paying up small debts and loans, and in some extreme cases, filing for bankruptcy, and of course changing your spending habits, among other factors. More often than not, repairing your credit involves calculated activities which you need to orchestrate by yourself rather than consulting a credit repair company. This book is centered on how you can achieve an excellent credit score all by yourself. Repairing your credit posits you for greater chances in the finance world, and helps you save more. To prepare your mind for the long exercise of credit repair, I provide you in the next few paragraphs what you stand to gain for fixing your credit and boosting your credit score.

First off, repairing your credit boosts your chance of getting loans at ease. In addition, you stand to get loans at very low-interest rates. A low credit score attracts a higher interest rate on the other hand. Loans aside, a high credit score also helps you pay less as premium charges for your insurance – life insurance, home insurance, auto insurance, and so on. Another equally important reason you need to repair your credit is to increase your credit limit. Issuers of credit cards look up your credit history to determine the extent of limit to place on your credit card. A good credit score boosts your credit card limit. No, that's not all that there is to fixing your credit. A high credit score helps you to pay fewer security deposits each time you have to register for one utility fee or the other. Telephone deposit charges and other utility service charges could be higher when your credit score is bad. More so, repairing your credit involves paying off your down debts, and this keeps debt collectors off your neck. If you have ever come back from work to meet a myriad of letters, calls, and emails from your debt collectors, you will understand what a high credit saves you from.

In addition, each time you need to rent an apartment, for example, or buy a property that would require you to pay in installments, or apply for a loan to start up a small business a high credit score places you at a favorite position for consideration, but a low credit score does exactly the opposite – it handicaps and frustrates you! The same applies to applying for a job and buying a car on auto loan. I must also mention the emotional and psychological dimensions of having a low credit score. With bad credit, you will always be required to get a co-signer for all of your applications for a loan or credit card. Getting one each time you need such a favor is not always easy. With a good credit score, you do not need to rely on co-signers for your transactions. Finally, it is best to be completely free from the pressure. It is almost inexhaustible how a bad credit score can wreck your life and leave you helpless. The only way out is to repair your credit and get yourself at a vantage position. The question is, how? This book is dedicated to helping you get out of your messy credit situation. With the right strategies properly applied, you can boost your poor or average credit score to 720 or more in a matter of weeks.

In this book, you will find all helpful information related to how to read your credit score, what to do to improve your credit score, what to do when you find any inaccurate information on your credit report, the perfect way to write a dispute letter, among many other core revelations credit repair companies do not want you to know. However, I start with the most primary basics of credit in the opening chapter. Are you ready?

CHAPTER ONE

FUNDAMENTALS OF CREDIT REPAIR

Repairing credit involves the crucial process of fixing bad credit, addressing legitimate issues regarding credit lenders, disputing wrong information with credit agencies, addressing fundamental issues as well as noting damages incurred from poor credit. Simply put, credit repair is the actual process of correcting or restoring a bad credit score. A credit repair can be done in a DIY (Do it yourself) manner or by contacting a credit bureau to point out incorrect information on a credit report as well as ask such information to be totally erased. To repair a credit obviously means there is a poor credit score.

What is Credit?

Credit refers to the trust which enables one party to lend out money or give out a loan to another of which the second party promises to pay back at a later date as agreed between both parties. In other words, it's the agreement between a borrower and a lender where the borrower promises to pay back at a later date with interest attached. Credit is also the creditworthiness of a business or an individual in taking up a new loan.

Credit Score

This is a numerical expression (usually a three-digit number between 300 & 850) based on the analysis of an individual's credit files used by credit card companies and banks to determine the creditworthiness of such person. Credit bureaus are the major source of a credit report which shows a person's credit score. Basically, credit scores are used by lenders to determine if one is worthy of a loan, how likely it is for one to pay back that loan, the interest rate, and the credit limits. The risk involved in loaning out money is determined through a credit score and if such risk should be taken at all.

For instance, if Mr. John's credit history containing his debts, types of accounts, number of late payments, age of accounts, etc., is really poor or too much on the negative side, with a poor credit score obviously, he's 70% likely to be refused a loan request. The highest or the more positive your credit score is, the higher your chances of getting your loan approved and the lesser of a credit risk you are to loaners.

Types of Credit Scores

- **Generic Credit Score**: This is a type of credit score used by businesses and lenders to gauge the general credit risk. It can be accessed through the same methods used by all credit reporting agencies.
- **Custom Credit Scores**: Unlike generic credit scores, custom scores are mostly used by individual lenders. Determining this kind of credit score requires credit reports, account history on a lender's portfolio, etc. Custom credit scores can be used by a particular kind of lending like auto lending or a particular kind of business.

Factors That Shape Your Credit Scores

The total amount of debts you owe, the different accounts you own/manage, the number of payments made late, and the age of your accounts are factors that influence your credit scores. There's however one thing you should note about credit scores. It's not limited to banks nor individuals alone but to other organizations such as digital finance companies, insurance companies, government departments, landlords and mobile companies.

Key Things You Should Familiarize Yourself with First

1. **Loan Review Mechanism (LRM)**: Also known as Credit audit, this refers to the act of examining the quality of a credit and also creating measures that can be taken to improve credit. The LRM evaluates the procedures for the deference of extant sanction and post-sanction as laid down by the bank. A credit audit is mainly to improve the quality of credit portfolio, detect issues early and suggest corrective measures as well as give a review on the sanction process for large loans.
2. **Credit Report**: This is a record or documentation of an individual's credit history from banks, agencies, government and credit card companies. The report is used by loaners to determine if a person should be granted a loan.

3. **Credit History**: Your credit history simply refers to a borrower's records of repayment of debts, loan refunds and how quickly they met up with their billing cycle across time.
4. **Credit Repair Software**: A software created by companies for their consumers to improve their credit score by themselves, correct wrong information and other errors found on their credit reports. It's a self-help software that enables an individual to navigate their way around loan qualification, tracking, credit scoring models, negotiations with potential creditors and credit score simulation.
5. **Credit Reporting System**: This refers to the connection of systems containing information of debtors along with legal, institutional and technological frameworks that give support to the databases in order to function in an efficient manner. The information can either belong to businesses or individuals.
6. **Credit Bureau**: A credit bureau is an agency set to gather information from different creditors about people's loan performance. This information may include previous loans that are already paid, newly acquired loans, how these loans are being serviced as well as any other outstanding balance(s). The information also includes contact addresses of the borrowers. The three major credit bureaus are Transunion, Experian, and Equifax.
7. **The Fair Credit Reporting Act (FCRA)**: The FCRA describes a federal law that regulates access to people's credit

reports as well as the collection of such information. The act was passed around 1970 to address issues concerning the privacy, fairness, and accuracy of personal information kept in credit reporting agencies.

8. **Credit Repair Company**: A company, an agency, or an organization that offers to boost credit scores and handle all works concerning working with credit reporting agencies in exchange for a fee.
9. **Credit Consultant/Credit Counselor**: This is one who helps an individual or organization achieve financial freedom. This set of people mostly work in nonprofit organizations that help people pay off their debts, manage their money as well as build a solid budget.
10. **Account Monitoring**: Otherwise known as Credit review, account monitoring involves the process of accessing a business or an individual's credit profile. This assessment is done by a creditor periodically.

What is the need for credit repair? Is it absolutely necessary?

Naturally, we need resources, one of which is money, to survive. Money determines and affects almost every area of our life. When you have a bad credit, you'll face different as well as difficult problems such as the following.

- **Loan Rejection**: It stands to reason that no lender is willing to loan out to individuals or businesses who have poor credit. Lenders like auto lenders and mortgage are hardening restrictions on new loans. The worse your credit score is, the higher the down payment you'll be required to make, the higher the interest you'll be required to pay and the higher your chances of getting your loan rejected altogether.
- **Insurance Premiums**: A bad credit or low credit score is viewed by insurance providers as high-risk behavior. This doesn't work in your favor. The importance of good credit cannot be overemphasized because the business side of risk mitigation is insurance of which depends wholly on your credit score. Your track financial record comes heavily into play when it comes to determining your risk level by insurance companies. No loaner wants to incur a loss.
- **Job Opportunities**: Due to the competitive nature of the employment market, employers employ credit checks as a measure to screen job applications. They make use of credit reports to determine the level of responsibility of a potential employee. In simple words, if you have a history of spending nonchalantly, you'll be less likely employed regardless of your excellent qualifications. You'll appear to them as irresponsible and disorganized, two things that definitely won't get you a job.

> **Savings**: When you have a good credit score, you have higher chances of starting your own business, retire relatively early, get a good education or be ready for any unforeseen eventualities/emergencies. The less you spend, the more you save, the more your chances of securing a loan on great terms and the less you acquire debts.

CHAPTER TWO

UTILIZING YOUR CREDIT SCORE, GOOD OR BAD?

The amount of credit used by an individual or a business compared to the amount of credit loaned to either of the two categories is what's referred to as credit utilization. Utilizing your credit is one of the two biggest factors that influence your credit score, the first being your payment history. You'll have to maintain a good credit utilization if you want to build a good credit score. If you have a high credit utilization, chances are that your loan request won't be granted. If it gets granted, you might have to pay higher interest or even make a larger down payment supposing you used to have a good credit utilization.

Credit Utilization Rate: This refers to the amount of revolving credit a person is currently using divided by the total amount of revolving credit he/she has available. That is, the amount you owe divided by your credit limit. Credit utilization = Your total debt/Your total available credit. To calculate your credit score, your credit utilization is part of the things that will be put into consideration by credit scoring models.

A Low Credit Utilization: a good credit utilization is that which is less than 30%, meaning you're making use of less than that 30% of your monthly credit. Your balance will have to be kept below 30% of your credit limit otherwise you risk a drop in your credit score which might be bad. The best credit utilization, however, is that of a zero percent. We know this is hard to achieve owing to the fact that as humans, we naturally have to spend more to live comfortably, but then, you must keep it at the barest level possible. A zero percent utilization rate means you're not using your available credit. Having a good credit utilization gives you higher credit scores which definitely boosts your chances of securing more loans like credit cards and mortgages with favorable/comfortable terms.

Managing Your Credit Utilization

1. Ensure your set up balance alerts so you can be notified when you utilize your credit past the limit you initially set. This is to curb your spending and to also keep a watchful eye over your balances.
2. Increase your card limit by asking your card issuer or credit card company to add to your card limit when you have a favorable change in income. You can also reduce your credit

limit if you switch to a job with lesser income. When your credit card balance is reduced, your credit utilization will be lowered to less than 30% or 30% aggregate.

3. Rotate your credit cards. Endeavor to spread the charges of the purchase you make each month over various credit cards. Although, this is not guaranteed to work always because some credit scoring models will rather evaluate your overall card usage instead.
4. Try paying your credit cards twice every month in order to keep your credit utilization in check. This will ensure that your card is paid back early down to a level below 30%.
5. Pay attention to when your credit card issuer passes across information to the credit bureaus with special attention to the date you make the payments for your cards. Your credit utilization will rise up if your card issuers report information about your account to the credit bureaus a few days before the end of a billing cycle.

A Good Credit Score

We all want a good credit score, so we make efforts to get that score. But when our efforts aren't paying off as expected, we become baffled. The question is, do you actually know what a good credit score is?

A good credit score is that of 700 and above. An 800-credit score is considered excellent which means you make a better credit which in turn instills confidence and cement trusts in lenders to borrow you their money assured that you'll definitely pay back in time as agreed. As earlier mentioned in the previous chapter, a credit score is what lenders consider before giving out loans to anyone whether you're deserving of the loan. There are two major types of credit scores;

Fair Isaac Corporation Scores (FICO): Your FICO score ranges from 300 to 850. Based on FICO scoring models, a credit score above 670 is considered to be a good credit score while a score above 860 is considered to be an exceptional score.

Vantage Score: The vantage score of above 70c is considered to be a good credit score while a score of 750 above is considered an excellent credit score. Vantage score model was developed by the three major credit bureaus namely; Experian, Equifax, and Transunion.

Benefits of A Good Credit Score

- ❖ Loans and Credit Cards: Your credit score is a huge factor in determining if you're worthy to be granted a loan and at what interest you'll get it. A good credit score does not only increase your chances of getting the best interest rates but also provides a chance to pay lower finance charges on loans and your credit cards. With a good credit score, you pay less interest, ensuring that your debts are paid off quickly and you are able to retain more money to save or use for other important things.

- ❖ Strong Negotiating Power: When your credit is high or excellent, you gain the leverage to negotiate more for a lower interest rate over a new loan or a credit card. It gives you an added advantage of more bargaining power, something you definitely can't achieve with a low or bad credit score.
- ❖ Security Deposits on Utilities Cancelled: Security deposits can range from $100 to $200 which can be such an inconvenience during relocation. Security deposits can be a pain when you relocate or move to a new home due to circumstances beyond control. But with a good credit score, there won't be any need to pay for security deposits when you change service location or create a utility service in your name. Less hassle, more advantages.
- ❖ Great Car Insurance Rates: According to insurance companies, people with a low credit score are more likely to file claims and they get penalized with a higher insurance premium. To put it plainly, you'll become a scapegoat for auto insurers with your bad credit score. Should you, however, have a good credit score, your insurance charges won't be much.
- ❖ Higher Limits Approved: Another advantage of having a good credit score is that it increases your chances of borrowing more money because your credit score has gained the trust of banks and other financial institutions. Your borrowing capacity becomes higher when you have a

high credit score. Loaners are assured that you'll pay back right on time with the agreed interest rates.

- ❖ Bragging Rights: Naturally, you'll feel good about yourself thanks to your good credit score. You'll be able to negotiate with lenders in complete confidence without desperation nor despair which might be used against you by the way. All you have to do is plan how to spend, spend less and save more.
- ❖ Mobile Phone Contracts: A good credit score ensures you are able to make a purchase of a phone by signing a contract at a discounted price without having to pay a security deposit. If you have a low credit score, service providers may not give you a contract and you'll be forced to opt for one of the pay-as-you-go plans with more expensive phones.
- ❖ Approval for Rental Houses and Apartments: Just like banks or employers use credit scores as a screening measure, so do landlords do to potential tenants. Your chances of getting a new apartment are considerably lower if you have a bad credit score that may or may not have something to do with a previous eviction or any other issue. With a good credit score, you don't have any problem in getting approval for a rental house or an apartment. Great, right? Yeah.

Maintaining a Good Credit Score

It's not enough that you rebuild your credit score, you have to ensure your efforts do not go down the drain by constantly maintaining it so it doesn't drop lower again. Here's how:

- Keeping your old accounts in other to maintain an average credit history
- Continuing paying your bills right on time.
- Keep low balances on credit cards, seek out a new loan only when it's absolutely necessary for you to do so.
- Use a mix of different credit cards.
- Try applying for a secured credit card if you don't own one. You'll need to make a deposit which will eventually become your credit limit.

A Bad Credit Score

A bad credit score is one that is below 670. A credit score between 300 and 579 is considered to be very poor/poor respectively while a credit score between 580 and 669 is considered to be fair. These statistics are based on the FICO score range. For Vantage score, a credit score of 601 to 660 is considered to be a fair credit score, a credit score of 500 to 600 is considered to be poor while that of 300 to 499 is considered to be extremely poor.

The lower your credit score, the lesser your chances of qualifying for loans on good terms. Bad credit makes it difficult if not almost impossible for you to acquire an affordable loan or any loan at all.

Disadvantages of Having a Bad Credit

1. **High-Interest Rate, Possible Rejection of Loans & Credit Cards**: A low credit score shows lenders that loaning out to you involves higher risks than someone who has a high credit score. Either your loan gets rejected or lenders charge you a higher interest rate. A bad credit score robs you of the chance to get important loans such as private/federal student loans, credit loans, mortgages, personal loans, and the likes. And if your loan gets approved, you'll pay more interest than normal. You certainly do not want this kind of burden.
2. **Required Security Deposits on Utilities**: It won't matter that you pay your utility bills on time. If you have a bad credit score, you'll be made to pay a security deposit so as to establish service in your name when you relocate somewhere else. The deposit will be changed first before the service is established in your name.
3. **Difficulty in Securing an Employment**: The job market is quite fierce. There are some jobs especially those under the finance or management industry that a job seeker to have a good credit score or history before he/she can be considered for a job at all. What they are looking for is how you manage

your credit. It's one of the ways to determine what the job performance of a potential employee is likely to be.

4. **Difficulty in Getting an Apartment Application Approved**: Getting a rental application approved with bad credit will prove difficult because landlords don't want to give their out their rooms to people with poor credit. If you do manage to get a landlord who approves your application despite having a bad credit score, be prepared to pay a higher security deposit.

5. **Cell Phone Contract**: You won't be able to get a cell phone contract if you have a low credit score. Mobile companies check your credit history just so they can determine if you're worthy of the contract. You'll either get a mouth-to-mouth contact with more expensive phones.

6. **Higher Insurance Premiums**: Insurance companies will always take into consideration your credit history to gauge your likelihood of submitting a claim. A bad credit score proves that you're more likely to file claims and as such, you'll be charged with higher insurance premiums. Suffice to say that there's absolutely nothing to gain with a bad credit score.

7. **Difficult in Starting Your Own Business**: Having a low credit score is no way of achieving financial freedom. Your dream of starting your very own business can't be achieved if you have a bad credit score. Regardless of coming up with a solid business plan along with supporting data, you might not

be granted the loan or the specific amount you need to fund your new business.

8. **Inability or Difficulty in Purchasing a Car**: Your car loan won't be approved if you have a bad credit score. Banks make sure they check your credit history first before they can consider your loan request and if it's bad, your request gets turned down or approved on the condition of a higher interest rate. The higher the interest rates with payment if you're purchasing the vehicle from a "buy here, pay here" car lot.

How to Check Your Credit Score

It's important to check your credit score regularly especially when you apply for a mortgage, new credit card or personal loan. It shows you the interest rates you're likely to pay when applying for a new loan. Not only do you have to check your credit score to determine if you qualify for a new loan, but you also have to check in order to be aware of any drop, mistakes or potential fraud you might be at risk of. When you make it a point to always check your credit score, you'll be aware of errors quickly and find ways to resolve them before they escalate to big-time issues. Checking your credit score is actually an easy thing to do. There are different ways of calculating your credit score depending on the scoring model. The criteria used by scoring models are different but they are all based on some common features you'll find below.

- **The Payment History**: This accounts for 35% of your FICO credit score and it's one of the most important determinants of your credit score. Lenders inspect your payment history to determine if you'll be able to pay back what you want to borrow and in time. Your score can be gravely affected if you missed just one payment.

- **Credit Mix**: Credit mix makes up about 20% of your FICO credit score. It's used by credit lenders to evaluate how well you handled your past debts. Those with high credit scores are known to usually have a portfolio of different credit accounts. These accounts are thoroughly examined by credit scoring models.
- **Credit Utilization**: It makes up 30% of your FICO score calculated by dividing the revolving credit you currently use by the total of your revolving credit limits. This ratio determines how you rely on non-cash funds and how much credit you currently utilize.
- **Negative Information**: This information comprises of missed or late payments, charge offs, foreclosing as well as collection accounts that are indicated in your credit file/report. Negative information on your credit file lowers your chances of getting approved for a new loan and they are info that stays in your file for a very long time, up to seven years. You do not want that kind of history on your credit.

New Credit: New credits account for 10% of your FICO score indicating how often you open new accounts.

- **Length of Credit History**: This refers to the length of time you've had credit. It accounts for 15% of your FICO credit score.

Calculate your credit score by logging in to your credit card issuer's site or any other free credit score service. Go to the credit score section, you'll see a dashboard showcasing your credit score and every other element affecting it.

The Credit Score You Should Check

According to John Ulzheimer, a credit expert, both FICO and VantageScore credit scores must be checked in order to get the full and accurate details of what loaners will see. Typically, FICO and VantageScore credit score from either one of the three major credit bureaus mentioned earlier.

Types of Accounts That Affect Your Credit Scores

Generally, your credit file comprises information on both revolving and installment loans among other things. Both accounts are also factors that influence your credit scores as they are records of your debt and payment history. Find the two types of the accounts below.

- Revolving Credit: is a type of account involving home equity loans and credit cards. It doesn't have a fixed term but has a tendency to fluctuate. It provides a credit limit where you make payments based on how much credit you utilize.
- Installment Credit: Installment credit accounts are associated with mortgages, student and personal loans where a person borrows a fixed amount of credit with the agreement to make a payment every month until the loan is totally paid off.

These two types of accounts are crucial to your credit score calculation.

Factors That Affect Your Credit Score Negatively

- ★ Applying for Too Many Loans in a Short Time: Having too many inquiries recorded in your credit file over a short period of time reflects poorly on your credit score. Lenders take note of every hard inquiry made in your file. If they are too many in a short time, you won't be granted a loan. A hard inquiry is recorded in your file each time you request new credit and the lender asks for your credit report before making a decision.
- ★ Missing Payments: When you miss a payment, even just once, it affects your credit score badly. Your payment history constitutes a larger aspect of your FICO. You might want to take serious care of this and avoid missing any payment in the future.
- ★ Accounts Default: Negative account information such as settled accounts, bankruptcy, foreclosure, charge offs and repossession on your credit report can affect your credit score negatively up to ten years.
- ★ High Credit Utilization: Typically, lenders prefer to see a credit utilization of 10% to 39% before giving out loans. If you use too much of your available credit, you're indirectly telling creditors that you depend too much on credit and lack the ability to manage your credit effectively.

Factors That Do Not Affect Your Credit Scores

Factors such as your income, net worth, balances in retirement accounts and equity in your home have no impact whatsoever on your credit score contrary to popular belief. Moving further, your assets, education, employment history, job title, nationality, age, and political affiliation are not considered for your credit score calculation.

Impact of Your Credit Score on Your Credit Cards

A good or excellent credit score gives you the chance to qualify for more credit cards (travel rewards card, chase sapphire reserve, and the likes) with favorable interests. You can also get the Discover it ® secured card if you have to rebuild your poor credit. The card gives you access to a credit card when you make a security deposit.

Impact of Having Different Account on Your Credit Score

Although, having fewer credit accounts won't actually affect your credit score negatively, having numerous credit accounts indicates your ability to manage different types of debts all at the same time as well as the ability to pay back such debts. It's also a factor that boosts up your credit score.

Impact of Service Accounts on Your Credit Score

Except you fail to make payments and your service account is referred to a collection agency, service accounts have no impact on your credit score. The service accounts might include phone bills and utility which by the way are not automatically added to your credit report.

How to Rebuild Your Credit Score

Rebuilding your credit score will take a considerable amount of time and a lot of effort. It's quite easy to do as long as you're focused and you're able to determine the reason behind its poor state. Here are the essential steps to take:

1. **Do a Check**: The first thing you have to do is get a free copy of your credit score and report so you can see what's in your file as well as factors that are affecting your credit score. In addition, it's crucial to check for negative information, inaccuracies that appear on your credit report, dubious accounts that are opened in your name. The following elements are key things to having a higher credit score that you must check for.
    i. Your payment history, which must always be paid on time without missing any of the payments for whatever reasons.
    ii. Your credit utilization rate, which must not exceed 30% if you desire to have a good credit score.
    iii. The duration of your credit usage which makes up 15% of your credit score.
    iv. The mix of credit accounts you have which gives you more chance of getting a good credit score.

v. The number of hard inquiries filed into your credit report, applications you've made as well as the number of credit accounts in your name.

2. **Pay Your Bills On Time**: By now, you know how important payment history is to your overall credit score. It's the biggest determinant of your FICO credit score, taking up about 35% of it. Try to pay all bills on time without missing any payments. You can set up an auto-pay feature for recurring bills such as mortgages, car payments, student loans, and the likes so you're always on time to pay them.

   You only have to make sure to have enough money in your bank accounts to cover for every one of your payments. It's not even necessary to send a check or log in to a payment portal. With the autopay feature, your payments are automatic.

   In case you have a lot of payments due on the same day, you'll have to contact your creditors to change dates. Inform them early if you're going to miss making payment before it happens. You do not want to look irresponsible or be accused of breaching the contract. It's important you keep a good relationship with your creditors.

3. **Pay up Outstanding debts**: Your credit file does not only contain information about your late payments among other things but also how late those payments are made ranging from 30-60-90 days. The more time of late payments that elapsed, the more the negative impact on your credit score.

Stop the use of your credit cards and try paying off your credit card debts first. Employ the use of the Debt Snowball method to pay off small debts. Also, try out the Debt Evaluate method which allows you to spend some extra money to the highest interest credit card. This helps you save the money in interest.

4. **Disputing Information**: Make sure to dispute every inaccurate information on your credit report because while mistakes might occur, not detecting them early enough to make the necessary corrections is bound to hurt your credit score. Always check your credit reports regularly to ensure that there's no wrong information on it. This is another great way of rebuilding up your credit score to a high level.

5. **Avoid Applying for New Loan**: To rebuild your credit score, you have to avoid new hard inquiries in which loaners check your credit report to determine your creditworthiness. If you keep borrowing without giving enough amount of time in between the loans, hard inquiries will keep adding up and that's definitely not going to help rebuild your credit score. Lenders will only see you as a high credit risk when you try to borrow from a lot of sources all within a short time.

Soft inquiries, on the other hand, happen when a lender or a credit issuer evaluates your credit to preapprove you for a loan. It's also when you as an individual check your credit score. You should, however, note that if you apply with more than three lenders in a short period of time when applying for

a mortgage or a single loan, there won't be any big effect on your credit score.
6. **Get Help**: You can get the help of professionals or agencies if you still can't do it yourself. You can also get help by becoming an authorized user on another person's account, get a co-signer with good credit or open a secured credit card account in which you place some amount of money in and you'll be allowed to borrow up to a specific amount of cash.

CHAPTER THREE

DEBT MANAGEMENT

Credit is actually the money available to be loaned out. It's the ability of an individual to take on debts serving as a kind of back up funds to provide you with the means of getting what you need. Credit is used to make the purchase of goods and services with borrowed money. A credit card company or a bank creates a credit account for you with a maximum amount of money you can borrow, making it your credit limit. The common sources of credit are personal loans, student loans, car loans, mortgages and credit cards. If your available credit is greater than your current level of debts, loaners will see you as creditworthy when you want to borrow. A credit card is a card useful for basic transactions where you sign on purchases with the exemption of gas payment, and pay interest on the purchases made in 30 days.

Debt, on the other hand, refers to the money that is borrowed to be paid back at a later time with a specific interest. It can also be said to be the result of borrowing money from lenders. Debt happens when you make use of your available credit. It's the actual money you owe, of which you're supposed to pay back to your creditors. To put it simply, credit is how much you can borrow while debt is the exact amount of money you owe to your creditors. A debit card is a card that allows you to make payment of purchases made by sending the payment directly from your bank account to your creditors.

Debts

Millions of people are neck-deep in debts of business loans, mortgages, personal loans, etc. It's rather difficult to stay away from debts or pay them off if there's no proper debt management. Most people find that the debts keep piling up, no thanks to the interest rates attached. They go into debt because they either spend more than they earn or lack the discipline to inculcate the habit of paying off their debt. It's in your best interest to seek out professional advice on how to manage your debts especially if you find it very difficult to repay them back. Consider speaking to your creditors too without delay so you can work out how best to repay these loans.

Why do People Acquire Debts?

1. Poor Money Management: This is a no-brainer, and probably the biggest reason people acquire debt. It obviously speaks for itself. When you don't have a proper budget or lack the discipline to track your daily and monthly spending, you'll surely move down the road to debt faster than you can think especially if you earn lower than you spend. Lack of budget invokes debt. You won't be able to curb unnecessary expenditures and you might have to take up a loan to keep up with those expenses.
2. Income: Sometimes in life, we get hit with unexpected changes like a job or income crises. There could be a problem at your workplace when workers' pay gets reduced or employees get fired. The sudden change in income or loss of a person's livelihood is another huge factor that influences people into becoming debtors. When people find themselves with a lesser income for whatever reason, they fail to handle such a situation accordingly.

    Most people can't deal with change, certainly the one negatively attached to their occupation. Failure to tailor your expenses in line with your low income thereby letting your expenses exceed the said income pushes you to take up loans after loans that you definitely won't be able to pay off. Not in record time at least. The key thing here is a proper budget.
3. Gambling: Here is another huge reason people go into debt. Due to its entertaining and addictive nature, those who

gamble are stuck with it helplessly. Gamblers can't seem to drop the foul habit. Sometimes, all it takes is just one try and they get hooked forever, gambling all their life away only to later turn up in the streets homeless. When the debts keep piling up without a way out, with an unbearable pressure from creditors/loan sharks, most gamblers are driven to crime.

Lenders play on gamblers' addiction, always offering to give out more loans even when the previous debts haven't been paid off until such gambler gets in so deep that whatever he owns gets transferred to his creditor. Gambling, however, is a game and a business, a dangerous one at that albeit entertaining as well as lucrative.

4. Lack of Savings: Not saving up for the "rainy day" is yet another reason people go into debt. When you have nothing put aside for future expenditure, expected or unexpected, relating to severe health issues, unemployment, death of a family member, etc., you'll have no choice but to seek out lenders. Having nothing saved can never bring you anything good but a burden like debt.

5. Medical Expenses: It's the 21st century where doctors and hospitals are charging much more over medical treatments. One can hardly blame them though. Those treatments are costly to make and the world is advancing more. While the high cost in treatments especially for severe health cases can't be blamed on hospitals, their growing impatience at people who are unable to pay up their medical bills on time is

appalling. It's another reason people get swamped in the very deep ocean of debts. Taking out a loan or pulling your medical expenses on your credit cards becomes so much easier when you don't have the money to pay for your bills.

6. Divorce: American laws rule over what should be done with a couple's money during a divorce settlement which by the way is another way a person can acquire so many debts. Should a party demand way too much during the divorce proceedings, the other party has no choice but to go whatever length to meet up with his/her partner's demands else he faces a jail term or a court fine. Not to mention paying off attorneys to represent his/her case. Divorce is seen by some as a gold mining.

Types of Debts

- Protected debt: This is defined by the need for collateral. It provides security to the moneylender that the borrower will pay up else risk losing the collateral placed on the line. The collateral can be a house, a car or any other valuable property.
- Unsecured debt: Here, the creditor's security is based on a high-interest rate that the debtor has to pay for along the principal loan amount. There is no collateral like credit card nor personal loans.
- Fixed payment debt: An example of this is mortgage which has the same interest rate for the complete timeline of the

loan. Mortgages are loans made to purchase homes with the subject real estate serving as collateral on the loan.
- Variable interest rate debt: The interest rate in this circumstance can vary over the existence of the loan just like credit cards
- Fixed payment term: Here, the loan is set to be paid by an already fixed date like student loans or mortgages.
- Variable repayment period: This type of debt has no fixed date when the debt must be paid like a credit card.
- Deductible: This type of loan is used to make personal conditions better and by effect have tax benefits just like in mortgages or student loans.
- Nondeductible: This is a loan that is not used in purchasing any asset skill just like in a credit card or a personal loan.

Signs Your Debts Are Getting Out of Control

There are certain obvious signs you have to watch out for to know if your debt rate is unhealthy and out of control. Some of which are highlighted below:

- You're barely keeping up with the minimum payments on your debt.
- Your debt continues to grow every month.
- You're no longer saving.
- Your credit score is not balanced anymore.

- Your creditors hound you for payments.
- You live on paycheck to paycheck and find it difficult to make a minimum monthly payment.
- You borrow money to keep up with paying off bills.
- You can't keep track of who you owe and how much you owe.
- You start missing payments.
- You're left with the need to choose between basic necessities or debt repayment.
- Taking out of your savings to pay your daily expenses.

What is Debt Management?

Debt management refers to the act of taking different effective steps and techniques aimed at paying off debts without too much delay. It's the discipline curtailed towards living your day to day life on a specified budget regardless of whatever caused the debts to accrue initially. Whatever steps you take or debt management service organization takes towards reducing and eventually paying off your debts is what is referred to as debt management. You'll be able to reduce the chances of sinking into debts and more debts if you take prudent steps that are surely bound to lead you down the road to financial stability.

Debt Management Services

There are various organizations (mostly working as independent counselors) out there who provide debt management services to debtors. The service is geared towards training debtors in finance management to help repay their debts within a short period of time, if possible, and depending on the kind of debt as well as the income of the debtor.

Debt Management Programs, How it Works and Things to be Noted

Debt management programs are programs designed by debt management companies to work with creditors on your behalf with the aim of reducing your debts through monthly payments, interests inclusive, as well as reduce penalties attached to late payments. By enrolling in the debt payment plan, you'll be able to make monthly deposits to creditors through a credit counseling organization using a payment schedule as laid down by the creditors and the counselors.

Pros of Debt Management Programs

- It helps a person stay more organized and punctual with payments.
- When payment is made regularly and in accordance with a plan, it reflects positively on credit reports and boosts up credit score over time.
- It creates a monthly budget that is realistic and has a steady financial goal.
- It offers credit card consolidation without a loan.
- Creditors and loan collectors will stop calling.

As attractive as these deals look on the surface, there are certain information to be known and noted. When considering a debt management plan, the following have to be put in mind.

- Make a Choice: Before signing up for the program, choose a credit counseling agency to help make the process easy. Some of the organizations offer nonprofit counseling for free, while others charge fees. They help in managing debt and developing a very practical budget. Once you find a credit counselor, he or she is to review your finances and help in creating a suitable budget. There are some points you must take note of when enrolling for a debt management program.
- The organization restricts consumers from using or applying for additional credit while enrolled in the plan.
- It will take up to 36-60 months to repay debt using a debt management plan.
- You can qualify for a lower interest rate on debts and a lower monthly payment.
- If debt management plans are late, consumers may lose progress on decreasing the debt and lowered interest fees.
- After deciding if debt management is good for you, the enrollment will be done by credit counselor who will work with creditors to negotiate the interest rate and come up with a payment schedule that is to be reviewed and approved by you.

Once the basic living costs including rent, mortgage, secured loans, and living expenses are paid, the money remaining will be divided among creditors. A deposit is to be made monthly to your credit counseling organization which will distribute the money to the creditor in accordance with payment already agreed upon.

Key Things to Note When you Enroll for Debt Management Program

- Making notes of debts and bills to be paid by the debt management plan and those to be paid by yourself every month.
- Paying a counseling agency on time each month.
- Reviewing monthly statements to ensure the counseling agency pays your bill on time and according to schedule.
- There will be an interview that covers all areas of your income, expenses, rent, utilities, medical bills, credit card bills, and other financial obligations.
- When the interview is in session, your credit information will be verified.
- Suggestions on certain areas where expenses should be cut down as well as where income should be increased will be made by the counselor.
- There will be an evaluation of the state of your cash flow and if it is still negative a solution of debt management program will be suggested.

- If there is an agreement to enroll in the program, a budget proposal will be worked up and sent to creditors for approval.
- You have to agree with the creditor on final terms involving payment and how long it will run for debt to be cleared.
- The bank account information will be asked for so that monthly payment will come automatically from your account to counsel's agency who pays creditors based on agreements already made
- The agreement is sent through the mail. Once signed and returned, the program begins.
- A monthly statement will be received by you from the credit counseling agency and creditor.

How Do You Manage your Debts?

1. Keep Records: The first step to managing your debt is to make a complete list of every one of your debts as well as the contact information of your creditors. Information regarding the date you borrowed the money, interest rates, monthly payments and due dates of the payments must be recorded down. This will help keep you in check, making you conscious of your debts as well as spur you into taking meaningful actions that will help manage your debts. Ensure you update the list each time your debt increases or decreases.

2. Always Pay on Time: Your debt will keep piling up if you refuse to make payments on time. If you're fond of making late payments, you'll only find it difficult to pay off your debts totally not to mention the fact that you might also have to pay a penalty fee if you miss a payment. You can set a reminder on your phone to alert you when it's time for you to pay off your monthly due. In addition, don't wait for another month to make a payment if you miss one before. Just pay up immediately you remember. You do not want to be reported to the credit bureau as such action is bound to reflect badly on your credit report/score.
3. Set Your Priorities Right: Ideally, the best thing to do is to first pay off the debt on your credit card since they tend to have higher interest rates than your other debts. Credit cards with high-interest rates will obviously cost you more money. Make a list of your debts according to their importance so you know which to pay first. Although, you can pay the debt which has the lowest balance first.
4. Put a Budget on Your Expenses: Draft a budget that will cover your monthly expenses so you don't spend more than you ought to and you can also keep up with the monthly payment of your debts. A budget will keep you on your guard as well as ensure you have some savings to be used for some unforeseen eventualities. Honestly, even without debts to pay off, people ought to plan their monthly expenses. It's an effective technique to prevent you from becoming a debtor.

5. Minimum Payment: Try to make the minimum payment you can afford even if you don't have the exact monthly payment you are supposed to make. While it won't be significant in reducing your debts, it definitely will keep your debt from adding up. It might look like a waste of time but it's better than not paying anything at all thereby missing payments. This will not keep your account in good standing.
6. Pay Charge-offs: Endeavor to pay off your past due accounts whenever you can so you can keep your account in good standing. If your funds are limited, focus instead on your positive accounts rather than those already affected with debts.
7. Create Funds for Emergencies: If you don't have savings, try, at least, to keep some emergency funds you can fall back on to cater for expenses that come up suddenly, expenses you are not expecting. You can always start with a low amount then increase it over time.
8. Know When You Need Help: When you find it hard to manage your debt, pay them off or you have a reckless spending habit, you should know that you need help urgently before your debt pulls you into misery. Seek out debt management agencies, credit counseling agency or a debt-help group known as Debtors Anonymous. Other ways you can be free of debt is through debt settlement, debt consolidation and bankruptcy of which will be discussed in the coming chapters.

Types of Credit

- Open Credit: This kind of credit associated with charge cards is very rare. It's the account an individual can borrow from just like a credit card, up to a maximum amount that can be paid back fully each month.
- Revolving Credit: The revolving credit refers to a line of credit that is associated with home equity lines of credit and credit cards, of which an individual is allowed to borrow from but with a credit limit of the amount you can borrow at any given time. Interest rates apply and monthly payments are required.
- Installment Credit: This is rather a loan of a specific amount usually having a fixed, regular, occurring repayment schedule. Installment credit is very common and may include loans such as personal loans, mortgages, auto loans, student loans, and the likes.

How Do You Manage Your Credit?

Aside from monitoring your credit report and credit score, the following are other ways to manage your credit effectively.

1. Choose the Appropriate Credit Cards: Don't be in a rush or greedy in choosing credit cards, not all credit card offers should be accepted. You should rather go for credit cards of low-interest rates, that have the potential for cashback or

rewards as well as cards with no monthly fees. It's in your best interest to avoid store credit cards. You must consider the advantages and disadvantages, the annual fee of credit card rewards against your yearly earnings for cashback. Take your time in choosing credit cards that best suit your circumstances and also note that while having a number of credit cards can be useful, it's not ideal to have too much of them.

2. Build Your Credit History: Try to build your credit history with your credit cards by paying off your balance on time and in full every month. If, however, you want to repair your credit history, endeavor to balance up on all your payments so your cards can be current. Should you have different cards that are spread out, try to pay off your credit cards as soon as possible without closing them down so it doesn't backfire on your credit score.

3. Ask for a Reduction in Interest Rates: Managing your credit also includes asking your card issuer to reduce the interest rates on your cards. Your request won't be refused if you're the type that always makes payments on time. You can also make a transfer of your money to a new credit card with no interest charged on it. But you have to first make sure to calculate the transfer charge just to ensure it doesn't exceed the interest rates that would have been charged. In addition, ensure you stop using your other credit cards when you transfer to the one with no interest rate so you don't acquire more debts than you already owe.

4. Abstinence: While credit cards are very useful, they also have the ability to hurt you if you fail to learn how to use them appropriately. Avoid using your credit cards if you can't pay off your balance every month in full. You do not want to find yourself too deep in debt that you might have no way of coming out.

CHAPTER FOUR

UNDERSTANDING BANKRUPTCY, JUDGEMENT, AND LIENS

Bankruptcy

Bankruptcy is a legal proceeding involving a person or a business unable to pay outstanding debts owed. Only an organization or individual that is unable to completely honor its financial obligation or make payment to its creditor files for bankruptcy. This goes to say that a bankruptcy filing is a legal course of action taken by a company or person to relieve themselves from debt obligations where all outstanding debt of the company is evaluated and paid from the company's assets. A bankruptcy process begins usually with a petition filed by the debtor or on behalf of the creditors which results in the court giving a debt discharge order in most cases. As legal proceeding goes, bankruptcy is carried out to give individuals and businesses freedom from debt they have already incurred and at the same time provide creditors with the opportunity to get their debts paid. It can be said to allow for a fresh start by forgiving debts that cannot be paid and at the same time offering creditors a substantive opportunity to get methods of repayment based on the available assets of a person or business that can be liquidated.

Theoretically, this can mean that the ability to file for bankruptcy can benefit a whole economy by giving businesses and individuals a second chance to have the utmost access to consumer credit and by providing creditors with a reliable measure of debt repayment.

Once there is the successful completion of a bankruptcy proceeding, the debtor is to be relieved of their obligation from the debt that has been incurred before filing for bankruptcy. However, it will be on their credit record that such a person has acquired debts before and filed for bankruptcy. This information is going to remain on the record for about seven to ten years depending on the type of bankruptcy filed.

Cases involving bankruptcy is handled usually by federal courts. However, it is worthy of note that decisions made on bankruptcy cases that are federal are usually made by a bankruptcy judge, inclusive of decisions on whether a debtor is legible to file or if they should be discharged of their debts. Administration on cases involving bankruptcy is most times handled by a trustee who is to be appointed in the United States by the United States Trustee Program of the Department of Justice so as to represent the estate of the debtor during the proceedings. There is no contact between the judge and the debtor except there is any form of objection made in the case by the creditor.

Judgment

Filing for bankruptcy relief will discharge automatically most of the debts including lawsuit judgment. If bankruptcy is to discharge a lawsuit, it will have to depend on whether the judgment creditor already places a lien on the property in question or more particularly the type of injury or debt the judgment is meant to be for. Almost all lawsuit judgment that is against bankruptcy debtors involve debts that are unpaid. If a lender can eventually obtain a judgment, the liability of which will make your wages go down or go straight after your personal asset just so as to satisfy the judgment that is left outstanding by the debts.

However, the good news here is that filing for bankruptcy can automatically clear out the obligation to pay back all discharged debts. Even if the lawsuit is inconclusive and yet to be resolved in the court, filing for bankruptcy will automatically stop it from moving forward. In most cases, if it has been established that the lawsuit was already settled and has resulted in a judgment against you, your discharge is still valid so much as to your liabilities in most cases. However, where a judgment is in regard to a debt that cannot be discharged, bankruptcy will not be able to get rid of it

Some specific type of debt is can't be discharged during bankruptcy because of the following; some certain taxes, student loans, debts acquired by fraud, duress, false pretense or misrepresentation, criminal penalties fines or restitution others.

It is important to note that a bankruptcy discharge will wipe out personal liability for all discharged debts but cannot automatically remove liens that have been placed on the properties before proceeding to file that particular case. Not all judgment lien can be removed through bankruptcy and for this conclusion to be reached it depends solely on the value of the property in question, the specific amount of the lien and other valuable attachments on the property.

Lien

A lien is an agreement that gives the creditor an ownership interest in the property. Lenders of money as a way of minimizing risk get the borrowers to make an agreement that if the debt is not paid as earlier promised, the creditor will have the right to take away freely any property as already agreed, sell it at auction and use money made from it to pay up the outstanding balance from the loan. In cases where the auction price will fall short of what is owed, the borrower will still remain responsible for the outstanding bills which are known as a deficiency balance. It is noteworthy to state that some liens can be created by operation of law. A lien of unsecured debt will come into formation after the creditor has sued the borrower in court.

Liens in chapter 7 bankruptcy will most likely wipe out responsibilities to pay up a secured debt also including deficiency balance. The collaterals cannot be kept unless what is owed is being paid. A secured transaction has two basic parts: a responsibility which involves an obligation to pay back creditors and a right that entitles a creditor to use the lien to recover the collateral.

Lenders are required to perfect their liens since a security interest agreement will not qualify as secured debt on the condition that creditor perfect liens by recording the liens in an appropriate record office. Filing for a chapter 7 bankruptcy is way better than just letting the property included go through repossession because it wipes out the obligations to pay the entire loan including a deficiency balance as stated already.

Judgment Lien

This is a court ruling that gives a creditor an outright right to the possession of a debtor's real or personal property if he fails to fulfill his contractual obligations as already agreed upon. This lien can be made against a person or a business. It gives creditors enough access to assets like debtor's property, business or real estate to satisfy the judgment. When a plaintiff obtains a monetary judgment, such a plaintiff will be known as judgment creditor and the defendant, a judgment debtor. However, judgment liens are nonconsensual because they are attached to properties without the consent or agreement of the owner.

Ways to avoid a lien include; repayment of debt when a debt is paid, a creditor will have to remove his lien by filing a release through the same place the lien has been recorded.

Types of Bankruptcy

Basically, there are two types of bankruptcy. They are:

1. Debt Discharge: This is simply the cancellation of debt, thanks to bankruptcy. Based on the Internal Revenue Code, a debtor must add into their gross income, the discharge of indebtedness after which a court must have discharged his/her debt upon meeting all conditions. However, if a debtor should refuse financial counseling, commits a crime, fail to fully explain the loss of his/her assets, provide false information during court proceedings or basically disobey the orders of the court, a judge can rightfully refuse to discharge the debt of such a person.

   You should note that not everyone can have their debt discharged and that the discharge of a debt can only happen if a debtor is qualified through chapter 7 or chapter 11 bankruptcy. The result of bankruptcy ruling is the discharge of a debt. A debtor can be forgiven debt if that debt is canceled or discharged. After the discharge of a debt in court, the lender forfeits all rights to collect the debt and the debtor is not required to pay anymore.

   The institution provides a Form 1099-C that indicates the amount of debt that was forgiven. This form must be reported by the debtor as a miscellaneous income of which he/she is required to pay an income tax. However, not all debts can be discharged in bankruptcy. Such debts include personal injury judgments, student loans, homeowners' association dues, child support, alimony, and tax liabilities. Debtors who are not qualified for debt discharge are those with high monthly wages and those with a large number of consumer debts.

2. The Payment Plan: This is a kind of bankruptcy filed under chapter 13, where a debtor and his/her lawyer submit to the court, a kind of repayment plan of how the debtor plans to pay off his/her debts in three to five years. This plan is dependent on the debtor's income, food, and utilities, tax, and healthcare expenses. Should the court approve the plan, the debtor proceeds to make the payments required as stipulated in the plan. If such a debtor is consistent with the payments, the remaining debts at the end of the three to five-year period will be discharged. The payments are made to a trustee from the bankruptcy court who then proceeds to pay the creditors while getting a commission too.

With regards to business, the two types of bankruptcy are;

- Reorganization Bankruptcy: This is a kind of bankruptcy filed under chapter 11 which is meant to help business owners who have serious issues with their business but still have regular income and valuable assets, reorganize the business. The business is allowed to continue its operations with the court's supervision of course. The creditors aren't allowed to interfere with the debtors during the supervision. Business owners will have to share their reorganization plan with the creditors providing them part of the payment. But if the creditors do not agree with the plan, they have the right to file a competing plan.

- Farming Bankruptcy: This is filed as Chapter 12 bankruptcy. It is a type of bankruptcy specially designed for farmers of the same family. It is to help the family reorganize their farming business as well as settle all their debts. The unpredictable nature of farming and seasonal moods are factors that are seriously considered under chapter 12 bankruptcy.

Implications of Bankruptcy

Before you consider filing for bankruptcy, you need to first understand how it works as well as the pros and cons. It's not a simple issue that can be done quickly but has a complex side only a bankruptcy attorney understands. It would be best if you find out everything you can before filing for bankruptcy. Find below the consequences of filing a bankruptcy.

Pros

- Discharge: Getting debts discharged is one major reason people file for bankruptcy. And when such debt is discharged, erasing all your debts as well as preventing creditors from collecting further payments from you, the debtor becomes relieved. It's one huge advantage of filing for bankruptcy. Though, not everyone who filed for debt discharge is granted. If you owe debts on alimony, tax liabilities or child support, filing for bankruptcy would be a waste of time. Such debts are not forgiven nor discharged.

- Automatic Stay: Here is another advantage to be enjoyed when a bankruptcy is filed. It is a situation whereby the person who files for bankruptcy becomes automatically protected from the creditors, as well as the property over the collection of debts. The protection stays until the court finally decrees the debts to be honored and forgiven or discharged. In a situation that involves divorce proceedings, the automatic stay might get lifted.

Cons

- Loss of Property: There's a possibility that a bankruptcy filer might lose his property if the court decides it's valuable enough to pay off the debt owed. This would happen if you include your property in your case to the bankruptcy trustee. Your creditor will have higher leverage in trying to get your property especially if you used such property initially as collateral.
- Credit Score: Another downside to filing for bankruptcy is that it decreases your credit score. Loaners will only see you as risky when they check your credit history because filing for bankruptcy won't in any way clean up your debt history even though your debt is canceled. But it's a better

option than acquiring debt. You can always rebuild your credit score later.

- Privacy: If you're sensitive about your privacy, filing for bankruptcy might not be for you, and this explains why you must make your research if you want to file for bankruptcy. You can either prepare yourself against the consequences or look for other options. When you file a bankruptcy case, every detail about your financial statements becomes public. In other words, anyone can access your personal information without your permission. The amount you owed, who your creditors were, your bankruptcy schedule can be assessed easily by anyone. It can be such a big deal if you cherish your privacy.

Implications of Judgement

When a lender files a lawsuit against a debtor and the debtor refuses to answer to the lawsuit, there will be an automatic judgment termed a *Default Judgement* against such a person from the court. Answering to the lawsuit doesn't necessarily mean there won't be a judgment against the debtor. Failing to show up in court over the lawsuit filed against a debtor is known as *Affirmative Defense*. A lot of creditors hope that borrowers ignore the lawsuit so they can receive a default judgment which is in their favor. If, however, after a certain number of years, the borrower shows up in court, the statute of limitations that prevents a lender from collecting debts owed will likely guarantee the borrower a win. Judgment can always be seen on your credit reports until its expiry date is due. It can remain valid for up to 10 years or more.

An Execution of Levy: This is a situation in which a creditor presents to a sheriff the judgment against a debtor so that the sheriff can sell off the debtor's property as permitted by a court order. Under these circumstances, it would be best for the debtor to avoid a judgment all together by taking effective steps needed to defend the lawsuits filed against him/her. Having a judgment in your credit report can stop you from getting security clearances, affect your finances or even prevent you from getting insurance. Try to avoid a lawsuit and if you do get one filed against you, don't ignore. Make an effort to defend yourself in court instead.

Implications of Liens

There are liens that are good for your credit, and on the other hand, those bad for your credit. Consensual liens(good), Statutory liens(bad), and Judgment liens (very bad). Any lender who allows you to make purchases through financing will require collateral which is often in terms of a property. With this collateral, the lender will generate a priority interest in the property you backed your line of credit with. If you're unable to pay back, a lien will be placed on your property. This lien can, however, be the consensual, statutory or judgment type.

- Consensual Liens: As the name already implies, they are liens a debtor consent to. It can be requesting loans or lines of credit. The debtor will remain the owner of your property if you don't default on your payment obligation. While it's visible on your credit reports, consensual liens do not affect your credit report nor credit score negatively. Because of this, consensual liens are considered to be good liens.
- Statutory liens are a kind of liens considered bad for your credit. When a contractor doesn't get the payment for work done, the government places a tax lien. It will be indicated

in the credit report and can last up to a number of years reflecting negatively on your credit.

- Judgment liens: This is the most severe type of liens. It can also remain on your credit report over a long period of time. It happens when financial interest is granted to your creditors over your property by the court so as to cover up for damages that insurance didn't cover for. Such damages can be a liability claim or a serious accident.

How to Remove Judgement from your Credit Report

Removing judgment is a complicated process and can be such a headache. You might have to remove a judgment if you're into real estate. This is because tittle companies, owing to the difference in laws of different states, insist on the removal of a discharged judgment before any real estate deal can be closed. You can remove a judgment first by vacating it, satisfying it and if you can't satisfy it, you can get it discharged.

- Vacating a judgment can only work if the judgment is a default one. You can "set the judgment aside" or file a motion in the court requesting that the judgment be vacated or set aside. That will be after you've stated your reason for ignoring the lawsuit filed against you in the first place. Assuming you weren't aware of the lawsuit, hence your absence in court, you'll be able to file a motion two years from the initial date the default judgment became active. If, however, you were actually aware of the suit but deliberately ignored it, then you have only six months to file a motion. The judgment will be vacated if your motion is successful after which you can contest the case. You'll have more chance of winning with that. All these will have to be done with an attorney's help.

- If you can't vacate a judgment, you'll have to satisfy it after which your creditor must file a "satisfaction of judgment" with the court. When settling a judgment, ensure that there is a clearly written agreement indicating what exactly you're paying and when it's to be paid. Your attorney must make sure that payments get a satisfaction of judgment filed.

- If the first two methods fail, you can get your judgment discharged through bankruptcy. Get a lawyer to help you file a bankruptcy petition so that an automatic stay can be put on the judgment and creditors won't be able to take any actions that will push you into making payments.

How to Remove Liens

1. Satisfy Your Debts: You can remove a lien from your property if you pay off all your debts in full after which you must file a "Release of Lien" form. This form represents a proof that you have indeed paid your debt. The lien on your property will then be removed. Generally, the following actions must be carried out although different jurisdictions have different requirements. Get the "Release of lien" form. Fill out the form

with the necessary information. Provide a statement of payments to show you truly paid. Get your creditor to sign the form with a notary present to witness the signing. Make the necessary payments required to complete filling the "Release of lien" form.

2. Get a Court Order: If you're sure that the lien placed on your property was obtained through fraud or coercion, and you can produce evidence to support your claim, you can request that the lien be removed from your property through a court order.
3. File for Bankruptcy Under Chapter 7: You can also remove a lien by filing for Chapter 7 bankruptcy. Almost all your debt obligations will be discharged and you get to retain ownership of your property. This method is also known as Avoidance and meant only for judicial liens.
4. Work Out an Agreement with Your Creditors: This is a very simple way to remove a lien on your property. You can work out an agreement of some sort privately with your creditor. He/she can either agree or disagree. It depends on the worth of your debt and perhaps, your approach. Sometimes a creditor will agree to remove the lien on your property only if you can pay higher interest rates and higher monthly payments.
5. Statute of Limitations: Depending on your state, there is a certain number of years that the lien on your property is valid on, and how long a creditor can file a lawsuit. If you wait for

the statute of limitations to run out, the lien will become unenforceable.

CHAPTER FIVE

DEALING WITH FORECLOSURE

Foreclosure is one of the most miserable experiences anyone could have in the financial industry. It is usually considered the highest cause of depression in credit operation too. From any perspective anyone might like to view foreclosure, it always ends up becoming a stage no business owner or private individual wants to get.

What does the term *foreclosure* mean? To begin with, it has been used to mean all manner of things in different contexts. It depends on whom you ask; a stock trader understands a meaning different from what the security officer understands. It doesn't get any easier if you ask an engineer or a grammarian. They all have what they think it is. In the credit industry none the less, foreclosure is used to describe a situation where the assets of a debtor are sold to clear his debts. That doesn't always happen of course, but a lot of times, this may become necessary in order to clear some, if not all of the debts.

As a practical example, a debtor who takes an auto loan, with the pact that the second he/she is unable to continue paying the debt as outlined in their regulations, the vehicle should be seized and sold to cover the debt left; the business mogul who took some loan and invested in some company's pieces of machinery but end up unable to pay; the traditional who drew a mortgage, courtesy of his company and got fired, became jobless and unable to keep up with his monthly payment, and so many others. Usually, sudden loss of jobs, investments or expected gains is the reason most people cannot pay up. In order cases, some fall to chronic illness and spend all of their life savings on it, while some others are simply trying to outsmart the credit company. For the last set of people, they suddenly realize there is no way they could keep up with the deal terms because it is choking the life out of them and taking a chunk off their payroll. In any case, they become unable to pay up and their assets stand the risk of being sold to cover up their debts.

More often than not, foreclosure is drawn on debts that are secured. This means the debtor must have added some of his assets as collaterals that could be usurped the instant he defaults. They are usually items that can, to a large proportion, cover up the debt. Foreclosure is usually drawn on debts close to close credit too. What's that? The kind of debt drawn on long and well-outlined debts. For instance, credit card debts are not close-credit. There is no specific amount the debtor owes each month, he/she only has the liberty to spend within their credit limit each month, and they may choose to spend or not to. In the close credit case, the precise amount the debtor needs is drafted, the stable payment schedule is drawn and they are expected to turn in some amount at certain periods probably monthly, bi-annually, and so on. That's the kind of plans on which tangible loans like student loans, auto loans, charges mandated by the court, etc. are drawn.

As you would expect, Foreclosure is usually outlined in loan contracts too. It is clearly outlined whether the lender or investor has all the rights to seize the asset the instant the debtor defaults, or there are other clauses to be fulfilled before such assets are usurped. In most cases, lenders are usually individuals or firms who have enough resources to cover up if the debtor defaults, though of course, the debtor is not expected to default. That's why in most cases, creditors involved in this are usually banks or very large credit companies.

Watching your property auctioned off in foreclosure isn't even the top of the problem; it can have a drastic effect on your credit score and credit report too – a situation that can spoil your chances of prospective credit transactions.

Foreclosure isn't simple. It isn't something your creditor can count hours after you default payment and sell off your property. It isn't something your debtor can hope to rope out of without feeling some effects too. The kind of effects and steps taken by both parties is largely dependent on the type of foreclosure drawn. This brings to mind the two types of foreclosure.

The two types of foreclosure:

>**The Judicial foreclosure:** The judicial foreclosure is the type that involves the court before a final resolution is passed on the asset and actions are taken. From my years of experience, debtors often prefer this to the next one we will discuss. But how does this work? The first step is to notify the debtor of his default

payments and allow him some time to clear his bill. That grace period is usually according to the earlier agreed terms of deals. If he/she fails to pay up, the lender is expected to proceed to a related court, file a lawsuit called *lis pedens* against the debtor. Immediately, the case is placed on the public record and the lender is usually allowed to auction off the asset(s).

Non-Judicial Closure: Fairly similar to the former, the non-judicial closure also results in the sale of the asset used as collateral. It is what is commonly called *Power of Sale* in the U.S. and the only difference between this and the former is that the lender needs not to seek the permission of the court before selling the asset. He/she has been empowered in the deed of the contract. The debtor is sent a note of default before any action is taken; the note is recorded in the county deed's office and the debtor is expected to pay up within a grace period usually between 3-6 months. If they fail to turn in the payment within the grace period, the asset comes directly under the control of the creditor who may choose to auction or reserve it. In most cases, assets are auctioned immediately. If the creditor reserves it, however, the foreclosure deal becomes known as *Strict foreclosure* in some states like Connecticut.

By inference, we may point out that there are two basic stages in foreclosure:

The pre-foreclosure stage: The pre-foreclosure is the earliest stage in foreclosure. It is the time between the period the debtor defaults and the time foreclosure happens. It includes the period when a debtor in danger of foreclosure is informed of their debts. The information is usually sent in the form of a note to remind the debtor of how much they are defaulting, and how, according to the rules of the contract they could forfeit some of their resources if they do not pay up. The total amount expected to be paid and the grace period, (the time within which they must pay up) are all found in this note. It foretells what is coming to the debtor. Foreclosure may be averted at this stage if the debtor tries to pay up within the grace period or, in some way, gets the creditors to negotiate a new deal that he/she could comfortably cover. The rule is that credit bureaus are not informed until about 30 days of default, at least, and the record may begin to appear on the credit report after the grace period.

The foreclosure stage: The foreclosure usually happens after the debtor has refused to pay up after the deadline given and has to pay the ultimate decision; let go of his/her asset. The style adopted to gain control of the asset isn't always the same. You will remember that it is defined by the type of foreclosure deal signed. The asset is usually sold within a week, and it is sold at a price usually less than the value of the item, first because the earlier it is cleared off, the earlier the investor got his/her funds. Then, poor upkeep and deterioration may be considered. In cases where the value of the asset has deteriorated so much that the money realized does not cover the total debts or the legal charges incurred in the foreclosure process, the lender may file a claim for a *deficiency judgment*.

What to do when you default?

Strike a new deal: Foreclosure can have a drastic effect on your credit card, and that's exactly why it may become necessary to involve every means possible. In many cases, it is realistic to open a new negotiation with your creditor. Let them see reasons you cannot afford to pay right now and propose infallible, and favorable alternatives. It's saved millions of people.

Right of redemption: The statutory right of redemption is a law that states that after a debtor has defaulted and the lender or creditor has taken control of their resources, the debtor may reclaim this asset. This may happen even if the lender has auctioned off the asset, as long as the redemption is done within the redemption period which is the period left for the defaulter to pay. Of course, that sounds weird for someone who hasn't paid the debt he/she owes, and that's why some terms must be in place.

In the first case, a debtor may reclaim his property if they pay up the precise amount they owe and the legal charges incurred in the foreclosure process. They may also retain their home if they participate in the auctioning which is usually announced on local radios for a fixed date, and then make the highest bid which gives them control again. If the cost of the house covers the debt incurred, the debtor would be permitted to own the house, but if they have more to pay, they would likely be served a deficiency judgment and would have to pay more. In most cases, debtors may make a profit by reselling the asset for a higher price, and they may pay off their debts with the profit. In the last case, a debtor may declare bankruptcy.

Declare bankruptcy: Declaring bankruptcy is the final resolution for anyone who can't afford their debt and is worried about losing their property. Often, people obtain secured loans using their most valuable resources such as houses or cars as collaterals. When they eventually realize they cannot pay up, they may resort to declaring bankruptcy. How does that help? They may retain control of the asset if the asset is considered one of the basic assets that cannot be lost in bankruptcy. Usually, that includes cars and basic company facilities. Notwithstanding, I must be quick to add that bankruptcy is the worst record on your credit profile.

You must be wondering by now, how bad can a foreclosure be on your profile? What harm can it do, if any? I am going to talk about that now:

EFFECTS OF FORECLOSURE ON CREDIT SCORES

Poor credit scores: We may outrightly begin with this. The most drastic effect that your foreclosure may cause on your credit report is poor credit scores. According to FICO's reports in 2019, you may witness a fall between 185 to 105 in your credit scores if you go through a foreclosure. There are speculations that the better your current scores, the more you feel the direct effects of foreclosure. Practically, you have just shown that sometimes, you do not even have the means to continue payment and your creditors might have to engage in property sales to get their money. Of course, you don't mean it that way. You did it because finances were tough and your creditors have to be paid, but it is the only way other creditors and potential lenders can read it.

You risk an awful record on your profile Having an awful record on your profile is a stigma you'd have to bear for quite a long while. By FRCA regulations, poor records such as bankruptcy, foreclosure, short sales are likely to remain in your credit record for a long time. By this, I mean until the next seven years at least, your credit report will bear that you have suffered a financial imbroglio at some point, that got so tough you had to give up some of the things you had, and that it may likely repeat itself. In the first place, it is hard to regain better credit scores, and you might have to spend a couple of years trying, at least. It is more difficult to erase this record even when you have better

grades. It is boldly in the section where your public judgments are expected and you can attempt its removal until 7 years after.
Higher charges for conventional financing: Now, this is one other problem. There are high chances that it will become pretty hard for you to get what others get easily. Lenders become unsure about your payment capacity, no matter what you present. They always want some cynical way to be assured. That is probably why you would be charged a higher interest rate when every other person. This might make it unbearable to obtain a lot of loans and you have to brace yourself up for that.

Getting a new loan becomes hard: You may regard this as the full implication of forfeiture. It usually leaves a bad impression, and it makes it practically impossible to get a new loan without stringent clauses or conditions. It is either that you need to pay higher interest or you need to put down some deposit higher than others do. You may also be required to fill forms that you otherwise wouldn't, but all that is if you are not turned down.

So you see, you must carefully consider your options before watching foreclosure happen. Particularly if you are at the pre-foreclosure stage. The long term effects are drastic and it may become too difficult to wipe off. You have every chance to avert it and it is always recommended that you try to stop it from happening.

CHAPTER SIX

THE TRUTH ABOUT CREDIT BUREAUS

Credit Bureaus are among the few organizations that can help you shape what happens in your financial world. Their presence, accuracy, errors, and general policies can affect your chances of getting financial support affect any person or firm in the world today. Without mincing words, it is okay not to understand religious organizations, social organizations or certain niches in the business world. But Credit bureaus? Nobody gets far in the business world without them. It is even wrong to start taking up loans and credits without having vital information on companies like these, and that's why I will tell you about them now. You will learn how vital they are to your credit too.

For a start, what exactly is a credit bureau? A credit bureau is a well-established organization that is saddled with the job of keeping and supplying related information on your credit every time you need it. They are usually called Credit Reporting Agencies because that's the top of what they do; report your credit. Credit bureaus or credit reporting agencies are usually specialized companies or organizations that take up the job of collecting, compiling and providing every necessary information on your credit when you need it. This is usually packed up and reported in the document formally known as 'credit report'.

Now, what is a credit report? It's a well-researched compilation of facts about your credit. The research is all done by your credit bureau; they only provide the details when you need them. They provide every related information that may help you decide how well you have handled your credit information. That would include some statistics such as your personal information, your credit information (the firms you have drawn credits with and what types of credit you have drawn), the previous judgments you have had based on finance, and your current credit score. You already have a good idea of what comprises your credit score.

Your credit reporting agencies are expected to provide you a free credit report once a year, and they may produce more than one on a charged basis. You may write to them to provide your credit information to certain companies, usually credit companies with which you are in a transaction already or from which you are about obtaining some credit. Credit Bureaus may provide your credit information when ordered by a court or the government, and definitely, your insurance company naturally gets a copy apart from cases where overviews of credit information are used in researches.

Your Credit Bureau would usually begin operation the instant you create a profile with them, and you instruct your credit companies to forward details of your credit transactions to them. For instance, you create a credit profile with *TransUnion*, a notable credit reporting agency in the United States. Then, you instruct your credit card companies to forward reports of your transaction with them to *TransUnion*, your credit Bureau. This means you expect your credit card company to supply reports on the type of loan you have drawn with them, how well you can pay up and their overall impression of your payment style. Such information would be supplied with your full name, the time you drew the loans, the time you are expected to pay it all, and clauses you have added during the deal. They are not expected to speak in your favor or against you, but only supply the information they gather about your interaction to the credit bureau.

It is the same thing when you take secured loans, you surely remember credit cards offer unsecured loans. If you draw up a student loan, mortgage or any other type of debt you may refer to as good or bad debt, you are drawing a secured loan. You may instruct your lenders to forward details of your transaction with them too. It is not necessary, but it is always advised since the next lender will likely lend you based on how impressed they are when they read and verify your previous debts, particularly how well you handled your last debt. The whole idea of credit scores and credit reporting centers on that.

Credit Bureaus do not collect all of your information, but are particular about only the pieces that relate to your credit, which will include statistics like "from whom did you draw credits, what were the policies agreed upon, what were the terms and how did you stick by them?" Your credit Bureaus then compile all of these bits and grade you on your performance in each and all of them. Some formats are followed when grading a credit report, and we will talk about every one of them in due time.

But we might begin by revealing more about the credit bureaus themselves. According to *National Finance*, there are three major credit reporting agencies in the US, they are **TransUnion, Experian**, and **Equifax**. *American Bankers* also report that these three are backed by different credit Acts in the US and they may request your credit records, your financial history, and certain personal information that may help them trace and compact your performance in credit dealings, even without informing you. Let's read up a bit on them:

TransUnion: If you'd like to judge them by the number of people they cover, TransUnion is the smallest of the three credit bureaus that are recognized in the United States, but it holds the widest range. It covers no less than 30 different countries in the world, including the United Kingdom. It provides demographic data and analytics alongside credit reports, and it is considered among the most reliable of the credit bureaus in the world. By 2020, TransUnion would be 52 years since establishment.

Experian: Experian was established only 23 years ago (as of 2019), so it is usually considered the youngest of the three by age. But nonetheless, Experian stands among the most reliable credit reporting agencies in the country. It is most popular in countries across Europe and of course the United States, and it has headquarters in world countries. It renders the same services as TransUnion, and it records information on more than 200 million citizens in the US alone.

Equifax: The oldest largest and most popular in the United States, Equifax is the third of the main credit companies recognized in the US. It keeps the record of well over 800 million people, besides millions of business profiles. Equifax holds an impressive record of credit keeping across all states in the US, and as such, it is often recognized as others.

According to *American Bankers*, the three organizations are charged with three major assignments — collecting your information, making an analysis of what they got, and making that available to due companies, and certainly, yourself. Every other credit bureau is charged with the same assignment, but it is worthy of note that about 100 other credit bureaus exist, only that they are rarely accessible to all citizens.

Each of these credit bureaus is expected to provide a free credit report to each individual on request. They must also present an avenue through which citizens may refute and challenge the statistics in their credit report. This means that if you receive your credit report and you observe some statistics that have doubts about, you may reach your credit bureau and have the error corrected.

How does your credit reporting agency get reports on your credit?

Credit bureaus require information, and they need to find it in some way. It is the only way they can have enough records to provide when you request your credit information, and they are protected by the Fair Credit Reporting Act in the US. This Act grants them the license to collect information on everyone they can and compile this information with the SS Number of each person. It is interesting to note that each agency has its method of getting information. This is why certain information may reflect in the report of a company and may be missing in the report of others.

Generally, what exactly do they need about you and how should they get your information?

The information credit bureaus usually require include:

Your data: The immediate data with which you want to be recognized is important. Your full name, your financial history, your social security number and so forth. It has to tally with what you have got on other papers. Credit bureaus try to see to it that your information is genuinely yours, and information belonging to someone with a similar name is not mixed up. It is worthy of note that credit companies or credit bureaus do not require your bank account details, your income scale or such statistics. They are only interested in what directly accounts for your credit.

Your credit information: This is one other important information credit bureau set out to collect. Your credit bureau gathers your credit history, your past and present credit deals and your commitment to each of them, as well as the rate at which your credit information can influence your credit score. It actually determines how high or low your credit score is, alongside a few other features.

Public Judgement: Public judgment can be an eye-opener for lending companies. If you have been vindicated in many court cases, it may prove to lenders that you are a brilliant debtor who must be venerated. It may also be the reason your lenders are skeptical if they realize you have poor public judgments, you have defaulted on many loans and you had to result to a range of alternatives before them.

Recent Inquiries: Lastly, the total number of firms that have recently inquired about your credit report is included in the credit report. The names and profiles of the firms, the form of deal you propose to them and so on are bits of information that your credit reporting agency may also set out to find.

So, how do they find all this data?

From your creditors: The most certain source of information is your creditors. They have records of how you performed in your debts. They usually submit a regular update on all of their clients to the credit bureaus, except in cases when the debtor requests that their credit information should not be sent to a credit bureau. In other cases, you may have to notify your credit company to supply your credit bureau with your credit information. Besides, public judgments and your recent inquiries, your credit companies usually supply the main information your firm is simple. Usually, your creditors are Credit Unions or banks.

The court: The court is another reliable source of information. The court provides a variety of information, ranging from public judgments to records of foreclosure, bankruptcy and such similar situations. The court naturally provides this information to the public record, and also sends them to credit bureaus the instant they are updated.

FICO and other Bureaus:

Apart from the fact that these credit bureaus rely on different sources to gather information about, they also use different methods to grade your credit score. These methods are known as Credit Scoring Models or Credit Scoring Format. Using those models, your credit bureaus generate a three-figure score between 300-850 after evaluating your performance. In most cases, your score is generated based on the occasion you need it for, and the value of the factors considered differ. For instance, your score when you apply for a bank loan may slightly differ from what you get when you request your credit bureau to send your credit information to an auto-loan company. Also, in a credit report, your medical debts may score higher than your auto-loans.

Of these models, FICO is the most popular, though fewer credit bureaus would rather use one of the others. What is FICO and what are the others?

FICO: FICO is one of the most reliable credit scoring models in the United States. It's been around for a long while and people have come to trust its judgment than that of others. It considers payment history, credit use, credit history and the type of credit above other factors when grading your credit score. It grades payment history more than the others, so it is your perfect bureau if you have an impressive credit record you'd like to formally set in your credit record.

Vantage: *Vantage* is another credit scoring model in the United States. By the records, Vantage uses the same range of scores as FICO (300-850), but it adds a letter range between A-F to help you understand and analyze your credit score. It rates payment history as 40%, unlike FICO which uses 35%, it is interested in how low you are able to keep your credit card balance, how regular you are able to pay and how deftly you avoid credit obligations when you can. Most of its statistics are similar to FICO's, but it is proving itself a better alternative and steadily increasing its audience over time. Its final results are closely similar to FICO's too.

Credit Xpert Score: This is one of the best credit score formats available to new individuals starting. But, contrarily, most credit lending firms would rather reckon with anything else. This credit scoring model proposes ways to improve scores on a credit report as much as possible particularly if the account is relatively new and the user requires some boost to stand a higher chance of obtaining a loan. It isn't very popular because credit unions do not fancy it.

TransRisk: *TransRisk* is often used when analyzing reports from TransUnion. Unlike the first two that emphasized history, it is more concerned about the chances of paying up the new loan. It emphasizes the wherewithal available and the individual's seeming capacity. Everyone often gets confused on one thing or the other about it, and as such, they do not usually reckon with it. You'd rather work with a clearer and simpler evaluation method too.

Besides these four, there are other notable models like the CE credit score model, Insurance score model, Experian's National Equivalency Score, and a few others.

The Fair Credit Reporting Act (FCRA):

The Fair Credit Reporting Act is a set of regulations in the US laws that state how credit should be collected, kept and reported by credit bureaus. According to title section 1681, of the US constitution where the FRCA is entrenched, the FRCA provides for the type of information that can be collected by credit bureaus, the kind of person or group who have access to these groups and the right of customers to reject a credit report in cases where errors are noticed.

What is the implication of that for you as a credit profile owner?

You and your credit reports are protected by the law.

Your personal information may not be provided to anyone without your consent except when such action is backed by law.

You have the right to accurate reports, and consequently, you may reject a credit report on the grounds of invalidity, inaccuracy or errors of any kind.

You have a right to free credit reports from these bureaus at least once in a year.

You may also call for negative reports on your credit profile such as bankruptcy to be removed after the deadline.

The Credit Repair Organization Act:

Credit repair organization Act is another regulation in the US that protects you and your company the instant you set out to repair your credit. From empirical reports, a lot of organizations have abused individuals based on their passionate desire to fix their credit and extorted them in every way possible. Many companies claim that they could create a fresh profile, wipe off negative information and do all sorts of delight on your credit report, such that your credit report becomes too good to be true. Fallacies like these are what this Act sets out to combat, and has actively combated since 1996.

What's the implication of this policy?

- The process of repairing credit can be handled by a person himself, so, credit repair firms must not claim that a credit report cannot be solved by the person himself.
- You deserve to be told the truth only, credit repair organizations must present only factual information to you.
- Credit repairing firms must not take advance payment for their services from you.
- Your contract with credit repairing firms must be documented and a clause that allows you to cancel the interaction at any time you desire must be attached.

CHAPTER SEVEN

DISPUTING NEGATIVE ACCOUNTS AND ERRORS

I'm sure by now, the most important thing ringing in your head is how important your credit report is. That's not even because it is yours, it is because it is a snapshot of your credit history. It reflects everything about your credit past, present, and as well, potentials. Everything, your bankruptcies, judgments, payment history, loans and credit cards that have ever existed in your name in the credit industry. I have to mention again that it is one vital element that can make or mar your chances of getting yourself a loan, and getting one in the best of terms possible. Due to that level of sensitivity, you want to make sure you have a perfect, impressive and impeccable report. Having a great record doesn't end in making the best you can in your credit profile, you know. It is not about paying up early, taking simple loans and all those tips you have heard earlier, it extends to double-checking and become confident that there is no iota of mistake in your credit record.

In a lot of cases, your credit record may be percolated with errors, probably from the information provider or your credit company. These errors can range from mild ones such as spelling errors to wider and drastic ones like errors in figures, names and so forth which may present a story that is not yours to anyone going through your credit report. Naturally, banks and credit unions would turn down your credit report when you have a name that does not align with whatever they have in their records, even in the case of spelling errors.

Once in awhile, errors can be a sweet thing on your profile. For instance, if you had defaulted four times and you find "once" on your credit report rather than 4, you would find that you have a higher credit score than you should have. Of course, that's a plus for you, but you shouldn't take advantage of errors like that. The error will likely be spotted, traced back and corrected sometime, and that drops where you should have been from the start. In point of fact, if it gets to this stage before it is corrected, the red flags on your credit report become obvious to your potential lender and that means one thing, you are putting yourself at a disadvantage because lenders may never trust your credit report.

In less dramatic situations, errors become the problem on your profile. If you have an average or high credit score originally, errors can begin to reduce your grade to such a bad score that you would stand no chance at getting a loan in the credit unions of your target. That's not even all, you will never be able to explain how you got so bad. You will doubt yourself and all the companies involved. "do I owe Bens Credit Union up to a thousand dollars?" you would ask dollars. They create doubts on your profile too, and persisting doubts are enough reasons to deny you a loan. This is why you have to consciously make efforts to have a good report, not just in practice but in writing as well.

However, there are times you find red flags that you cannot explain. You find confusing mix up of names on your credit profile, cleared loans or debts reappearing as loans and so forth. Sometimes, what you find are negative records like bankruptcy that have reached their exclusion period, and you have written a formal request to have them removed but for no official reason, they are still sitting in your credit report, staring you straight in the eye. You might come across trivial ones in your own case. But make it a point you would always remember, you cannot afford to have any errors on your report. Its effects can be drastic than you could ever imagine. You may get punished or deprived of various benefits due to the wrongs you never did, and it could bring you a range of legal, financial, and certainly economic implications. You must do everything possible to get them out of your credit profile immediately. You can read a step by step guide on how to do that in the next few lines, but before that, what exactly are those errors you may find on your credit errors and you should kick against them the instant you spot them?

Credit Errors can be recorded in the following areas:

    a. **Personality Error**: According to a release by *American Banker* in 2017, personality error is the most common form of error on a credit profile. It mostly involves errors made on the personal information of a credit report owner. Starting with your name. It is quite possible that your name wasn't well arranged on one or some of your credit transactions, or on your full credit profile. Other times, it is misspellings, or omission of some sort. It is even possible that an extra name is added to your original name, or a new name is introduced to substitute one of yours. Besides the name, you should check for your home address, business address, telephone, and mobile contacts too. See to it that they are accurate. Your social security number falls into this category.

    There are very high chances that somebody was lackadaisical, or was in a hurry when chipping these bits of information, as such, they could mix the figures or letters up and provide a piece of inaccurate information. They could go on to mix your profile up with that of someone with a similar name, and worst, this section of your credit profile would be the first target of anyone trying to hack your account. Particularly if they are looking to usurp your account. Checking the first part of your credit report is all you need to decipher these.

b. **Inaccurate account update**: This is another kind of error you must ensure does not occur on your profile. More often than not, this error occurs from your credit bureau or from your information-providing company (the firm providing that piece of information; your credit union credit card company, court, et cetera). Once in awhile, hackers may dabble into this too. We are talking about the part where details of your transactions are computed. Does your bankruptcy report still reflect when it shouldn't anymore, have you paid some debt and it still reflects as unpaid, or are the accounts you have closed still reported as open, did you find withdrawals you didn't make in your credit report? Do not try to assume they are yours. Pinpoint them immediately and take the necessary steps to get them out of your records. There is a street assumption that the instant you request for correction of errors or negative reports on your profile, your credit score will be reduced by the credit bureau and that's another minus. But throw that claim in the garbage, it's just another fallacy. If you are sure the stats aren't yours, go right on and request, your credit scores can only remain the same, or get better.

c. **Data Management Errors**: This type of error is similar to the previously discussed error. You are checking them up in the credit second segment of your credit report where details of your credit transactions are recorded too. It is something to make sure the account is up-to-date, it is another to have the assurance that the data provided tallies in all areas. Aren't there imbalances, wasn't any information reported twice or more, weren't the companies mixed and did the amount specified in each case tally with what you have always believed it is? Mistakes could be from anywhere and you should feel no reluctance when you are sure what you sure wasn't accurate and you must complain.

d. **Balance Report Errors**: now this is the business part. The whole idea of credit is hinged on facts and figures. The figures and facts presented on your credit profile are not likely accurate. This is because there is a lot of calculation to be done. From each credit transaction to the other, from the percentage impression in one to the other, and so on. You have quite a lot to calculate and you would be much safer if you take the rigor and calculate it yourself.

Summarily, errors may reflect in your personal, banking and credit information. They may also reflect in the manner that your data was presented. There are no small errors, and it usually makes a lot more sense to clear off the errors the instant you find them. That's the only way to avert upsetting situations that can put a question mark on the integrity of your company and your financial career.

Now, how should you go about correcting your credit report errors, here are the steps:

a. **Fish them all out**: my top recommendation is that you find out every error in your record before anything else. If you have just found one, there are high chances that there is one more somewhere at least, and you can draw up inferences from the new one you found. For example, you found an error in the details of your credit transaction with A&G Bank, your name was poorly spelled. There are chances that the figures in that transaction are wrongly provided too. For example, you may find $3,100 rather than $1,300. In other cases, looking further can prove to you that that the name was wrongly arranged in the other transactions too.

Whatever the case may seem, you can easily trace the dots when you examine your credit report thoroughly. A single error may have been made, but you are not going to allow one or multiple errors to ruin your financial opportunity, and that's why you would sit and fish it all out yourself.

b. **Contact the Information Provider when neces**sary: Even though credit-reporting agencies are liable to making errors, records prove that errors are not made from them a lot of times, the errors originate from your information provider. Your information provider is that the company expected to provide details of a particular record about or relating to your credit.

That is why in some cases, your information provider could be the Public record, the court, your bank or credit card company, your auto loan company or credit union. A few other firms may be involved in other cases. So, there are chances that this error has been made while your information provider was computing and providing information to your credit bureau. The pattern of the errors on your credit report can also give you a hint on where the errors started. This is when it becomes recommended to contact them first. Notify them and make inquiries, in order to ascertain the source of the error. It is also faster since you may get a response in a few hours while a credit bureau would take days to respond at least. You should bear in mind, however, they are not always guilty and it would be wise to thoroughly examine the reports, and having a solid opinion that the errors have something to do with them before getting them into the business. At those times you are not sure who is guilty, remember there's no harm in reaching out to them.

c. **Contact your credit bureau**: At those times you are sure your credit bureaus do not own the faults, you necessarily have to contact them. First, they supplied the information and it would continue to be in their records. If you have to contact them at times they own no-fault, how about those times you are sure this is entirely their mistake?

Just like it happened to Equifax in 2015, credit bureaus are fairly susceptible to constant attacks by hackers and there are chances that someone would access some bits of information, no matter how secured the system is. This is why it is quite imaginable that something was different on your credit report and it wasn't the same as the usual report you get from your credit company. In fact, you may get similar reports from two credit bureaus while for no official reason, you get different information from the third company. This is all on the same credit transaction that you have full records of, and that tallies with the report of the first two firms.

In a situation like that, it becomes crystal clear that the credit bureau owns the blame. Either you discover the error originates from the credit report agency or not, it becomes necessary to contact them and inform them of the error. How do you do that? We will definitely talk about that. As long as you send the required data, you can expect them to begin an investigation, compare the stats they have with the information they were provided and correct the stats if necessary if otherwise, all necessary information providers are contacted. If your information provider admits fault, a copy of their notification may be included in your enclosure to your credit bureau.

d. **Look forward to your credit report**: Correcting your credit reports would take any time around 30 days. After which your credit bureau would reach you, usually with another copy of your report, for free. If they found out the errors you pointed are errors in truth, they would supply a corrected copy, and if otherwise, they would supply another copy of your old credit report, stating that they had conducted researches and confirmed from your information providers, but there are no errors. You may at this point decide to sue your credit bureau, or drop things as they are, all on what you think about the new report.

e. **Further legal actions**: In most cases, the errors are identified and corrected, and your revised copy is forwarded in a few days. Afterward, your credit bureau is required by law, to contact every credit union and such other organizations that have been issued the inaccurate report within the past six months and notify them of the update in your account. Anyone who has received this credit report within the last two years must be sent the new copy.

As long as you take these steps into cognizance and ensure that in some way, every one of them is accomplished, you can correct the errors in your credit report. But how do you contact your credit report?

This is quite technical. There are tens of thousands, if not hundreds of thousands of people who are writing to correct errors at the same time. A lot of these people do not get a new credit report because they could not express themselves in clear terms, they were too livid to point out the main things they were, they provided inadequate information and in other cases, sent their report to a wrong address. These are the reasons the Fair Crediting Reporting Acts (FRCA) gave a specific format for the correction of credit report errors. This format must be followed when preparing and submitting a letter for the correction of errors. I have attached the format and some samples for your perusal:

[Your Name]
[Your Address]
[Your City, State, Zip Code]

[Date]

Complaint Department

[Company Name]

[Street Address]

[City, State, Zip Code]

Dear Sir or Madam:

I am writing to dispute the following information in my file. I have circled the items I dispute on the attached copy of the report I received.

This item [identify the item(s) disputed by name of the source, such as creditors or tax court, and identify the type of item, such as credit account, judgment, etc.] is [inaccurate or incomplete] because [describe what is inaccurate or incomplete and why]. I am requesting that the item be removed [or request another specific change] to correct the information.

Enclosed are copies of [use this sentence if applicable and describe any enclosed documentation, such as payment records and court documents] supporting my position. Please reinvestigate this [these] matter[s] and [delete or correct] the disputed item[s] as soon as possible.

Sincerely,

Your name

Enclosures: [List what you are enclosing.]

As you would agree, this is pretty forward and simple. The team understands you are upset about your records, but you need not invent new words to express your dismay, sticking to this guide raises your chances of getting a response before anyone who doesn't. In case you are unsure how to fix the words exactly, here's a guide:

This report if for Han Martinez who has just received her credit report from Equifax. She found out that the total amount left to pay her First City Union, her crediting company wasn't what she found in the record. I found $9,000 on her credit report and all there was to pay was $4,500, having paid $4,500 in the previous month. Here's what she writes:

Han Martinez,

2245 De La Boulevard Santa Clara CA

408

18/12/2019

Complaint Department

Equifax

P. O. Box 740241, Chester, PA Business Bureau Rating

Dear Sir or Madam:

I am writing to dispute the following information in my file. I have circled the items I dispute on the attached copy of the report I received.

The total amount left to pay "First City Union", my credit company is inaccurate because I have $4,500 left to be paid on my credit, and not $9,000. I am requesting that this error be corrected to the appropriate information.

Enclosed are copies of my receipts from the previous payments, my total charge and how they have been paid. I have also attached a copy of the most recent notification from First City Union, clearly stating my position that I have only $4,500 to balance. Please reinvestigate this matter and correct the disputed item as soon as possible.

Sincerely,

Han Martinez

Enclosures: [a receipt from First City issued on the 30th of December, My credit transaction from First City Union]

Hard? No way, I have a feeling you want to try drafting some right away.

CHAPTER EIGHT

TRUSTED TECHNIQUES FOR REPAIRING YOUR CREDIT

No matter how bad your credit is, you can restore it to one of the best credit profiles anyone could ever have. Your previous experiences, negative information, poor public records can all be muted such that you would have a credit profile that would reflect very high grades and impressive information. You can do all of these yourself, and you need not hire a credit repairing organization for it. In most cases, people have performed better when they try to repair their credit profile themselves rather than hire a credit repairing organization. That's to give emphasize the point that it is actually better to repair your credit yourself, and there is practically nothing special that credit repair companies have to do on your credit that you cannot do yourself. You may choose to hire them if you firmly believe you need their services, but if you'd like to work it out yourself, the techniques you should look to apply will be discussed in the next few lines. You should note that these techniques are the same as what your credit repair companies would take, and rather than speed things up, it can only get complicated with them. The techniques are listed below:

> **Brace up to repair your credit**: One important lesson that creditor counselors would never forget to bring is your mindset. Interestingly, most other people who would advise you in the industry may never bring up this suggestion. Instead, they could go straight to the other steps they consider necessary. But as important as the others, controlling your mindset is vital to repairing your credit. You must keep in mind that before anything else, your credit report must be repaired, your score must be fixed and you must build an impressive profile again. Bearing that in mind every time can help you decide how you guide your finances, what you purchase, how you set your budget and how you go by it. That's not all! It can help you draft

an opportunity cost table on which credit company should be paid when the month ends and who need not be paid. As a practical example, if you earn $600 each month and you have a monthly auto loan due of $100 and a credit card due of $150, it is easy to pay one of these and perhaps half of the other and then reserve your income for some other items on your budget. But if you build a strong mindset that all you want is to repair your credit profile, then before anything else, you would pay off your credit dues each month. Your level of commitment can also help you to build strong support from your creditors. So, before anything else, have your mindset on it, and believe that you can do it!

Become familiar with your credit report: It isn't inspiring to hear that your credit score became low because you had no idea what was going on in it but it would continue to happen if you do not become conversant with the updates in your credit record. Some do not request their credit report until a credit company demands it of them. That shouldn't be the case. Not only do you need to regularly update what you know about your credit report, but you also need to make incisive decisions based on what you gather. The first step is to become more familiar with your credit bureaus. Ensure you request your credit report from them. You have a right to a free copy annually and you may pay a token to get more. For example, if you get your free credit report in March, you may pay in July, and November to get updated ones.

The charges aren't usually high, but they are remarkably different. If you really mind the charges and you'd like to find some way around it, then take the rigor to read books that can guide you to learn how to calculate your credit report yourself. Be sure you scrutinize your credit reports for errors too.

Hire an Adviser: It may be a brilliant idea to hire a credit repair company, though you can do all there is to do yourself. Even if you do not hire a credit repair company, you definitely need some related experts. There are different fields of expertise in the financial industry, and you will move better with some of them at your service. For instance, you may hire a credit counselor. A credit counselor is a trained professional who keeps guiding you in your financial decisions. He/she offers you expert opinions, insightful plans, timed calculations, and so many others. Usually, a credit counselor can help you draft a fantastic budget too, and they may propose plans that can get you out of your condition much earlier than you would on your own. Credit counselors do not even have to sit with you all day. Their services are mostly online and you may choose to work with an NGO or a paid company. Besides credit counselors and credit repair firms, debt counselors, economists, financial experts, etc. are people you can bring into your financial journey.

Learn from your history: If you ask anyone in any field, you will discover that the only essence of history is to learn from it. Your history is your perfect display of what would be the result if you make the decisions you made in the past. Now, is your financial history satisfactory? I really do wonder if you would have to repair your credit at all if you had such an impressive history. You would agree that something went wrong or some decisions weren't right and that's why you ended up with such a bad credit score that you have to learn how to do it again. That is exactly what you should learn from history You need to make a thorough analysis and find it out. What was it that wasn't done right? What was it that should have been done more? What do you discover during your earlier times of exploration? Your history is your guide, be sure you make the best of it. But take note of this; you must not spend all of your life trying to evaluate your history. What was wrong is wrong already, and what was right no longer matters. Your concern is the future. You shouldn't reflect or dwell in your history so much that it becomes your priority. Common, the business is in the future!

Do not close your old credit account: A lot of times, business owners think their old credit profiles are excruciating or are sources of sadness and they really do not want to hear a thing about it anymore. Even though they cared so much about it, they made impressive records before something got wrong with it. Some do not just want anything related to the past in their new life, so they would shut down their old credit accounts. But is that always the solution? Absolutely not. More often than not, closing your old credit subtracts scores from your credit reports.

How? Your old credit account is proof of your experience. It is an establishment of how much you have delved your hands in the industry, made records, made mistakes and have learned from the whole story. It presents you as a veteran and you know that's a plus on your credit profile. That's not even all if you close the account and you have some damning record in it earlier, perhaps uncompleted loan payments and such records, it may get transferred to your new account and that's the worst thing anyone could ever start with. Whether you have unpaid credit records or not, why close your credit record at all?

Build great relations around the credit world: It is vital to build useful relations around your credit world, first with your relatives and friends. You need to build strong relations so well that they may consider you an authorized user of their credit. That could be a boost on your profile, particularly if your partner has an impress credit history. That credit profile will be referenced when considering yours since it is one of the credit profiles you directly have access to. From another perspective, you should look to build strong relations with your credit company too. Be sure the company understands your income and ability, and they can vouch for you if it ever comes to credits. It is the only way they would have less difficulty bearing things with you if you suddenly become incapable of paying your dues. Besides that, you can count on them to exclude a lot of negative marks before forwarding your record to the credit reporting agency. It is also recommended on applicable situations to build human relations, beyond company relations with key characters in your credit company.

Clear off your negative marks: Another worthwhile suggestion is that you should ensure you clear off all disheartening and downgrading records on your profile. Once in a while, the negative marks on your credit score are not actually earned by you; they could be errors from the credit bureaus and credit repair firms understand that. Credit repair firms are quick to spot this and that is why they could assure they would clear off your negative marks beyond what you could ever dare. It's all fallacy, it is nothing you cannot handle. You only need to find out what the source was. You may reach your credit bureaus or your credit company, you may also clear it off with much better performances. In remote cases, your negative marks are factual reports of your interaction. It is probably due to late payment or similar factors. You may contact your credit company to assist you in this regard. They may be sympathetic to your cause because you offer them a much better deal which they appreciate or you have better relations with them. In any of these cases, you may look to them to clear off that record.

Revere your old deals: If it was the case that you got out of your old debts with special help such as bankruptcy, debt management plans, forfeiture, and such other policies, see to it that you stand by every policy and regulation you have assented to in the deal. It is always advised that you consent to regulations you can bear comfortably. You must also see to it that all regulations are firmly followed and your monthly payment discharged when due. You may gradually repair your credit score using this method. In some cases, you may realize some clauses or payment methods are inconvenient. It is necessary to seek your credit company or intermediaries (depending on the type of plan you have used) immediately and sort things out with them. Don't wait till you default before you take action.

Request an increase in your credit limits: It is always recommended that you request an increase when you are starting again. As you would guess, credit card companies understand that it means an increase in their monthly profit, and would likely give a positive response. They may only hesitate on the grounds of poor credit history. If you can achieve it, however, it must ring in your mind that you must not spend beyond your usual credit on any occasion. You have only requested this to prove that you could have a larger amount at your disposal. In most cases, paying up the little you use is not difficult and your use of a less ratio is regarded as being penny-wise, and gain some extra marks on your profile. Positive marks like this can tremendously boost your credit scores and wipe out your negative records.

It is important to note as you keep trying all attempts you can, that the solutions are not magical. They would require a different length of time to resolve and boost your credit scores again. So, you would need to be really patient. With patience, careful consideration of these techniques and appropriate application, you would have your account bouncing with vibes again in the nearest future.

CONCLUSION

FINAL DIY IDEAS AND TIPS TO BEAR IN MIND AS YOU REPAIR YOUR CREDIT

So far in the journey of your credit repair, you have been exposed to a series of ideas, concepts, and strategies you need to carry out to make your life better. It is no more news that your credit score affects your life all round, even in ways that you never imagined. It could be a roadblock to opportunities that could change your life forever, and, at the same time, could be the access point to the good life you have always hoped for. It all depends on the state of your credit. In this concluding chapter, I present to you the tricks and tips that credit repair companies do not want you to know. These are tested and trusted measures to keep at the back of your mind as you go through the process of repairing your credit.

You Can Do It Yourself

This is the most foundational truth that credit repair companies do not want you to realize. It is true that the process involves some technicality and therefore requires some measure of tactics to see through, but this is not to say you cannot do it all by yourself with the right information. As a matter of fact, it is highly advisable to personally address your credit issues so as to keep you informed on the basic areas where you need to pay more attention to your day-to-day transactions. The right place to start is to request your credit report from any of the major credit bureaus and carefully analyze it yourself.

Pay up your Credit Cards Close to their Limits

No, you cannot just pay back your debts at random. It is highly recommendable to check out which one(s) is/are close to their limits and offset them first. The logic is simple: paying off credit cards that are close to limits magically reduces your utilization rate, and this holds a significant position in your credit report.

Increase your Payments Per Billing Cycle

Do not forget that the aim is to speed up the payment of your down debts and increase your creditworthiness. You also want to lower your utilization and boost your score. If you can afford it, double your bill payments per month.

No, you Don't have to Close your Credit Accounts

It is a common practice to find credit repair experts and companies as well as individuals wanting to close their credit accounts sometimes just after offsetting the debts on it. This is completely needless and does your credit report more harm than good. The truth is, closing an account does not remove it from your credit report. As a matter of fact, all the available details about the closed accounts are listed on your reports. On the contrary, leaving it open, even though you do not intend to use it, makes it a testimony to your payment history. Rather than close an account that gives you problems, you can transform it to your good by paying it off, however slowly. If at all you must close an account to reduce the excessive workload in you, it is recommendable to close the new ones with less history.

Sometimes, Doing Nothing Could be a Strategy

This is a very higher-order truth that nobody wants you to know. Its efficiency is highly dependent on the context and situation at hand anyway. Negative information will not always remain on your credit report; they have a duration of only about seven years although chapter seven bankruptcy can stay longer than that. Leaving negative information on your account to fall off, especially if the limit time is already close by is a wise approach. This is essentially helpful because every information, whether positive or negative, except for a few cases, falls off your credit account after seven years.

Focus on your Credit Utilization

It is important to pay adequate attention to your credit utilization. This refers to the percentage of credit you use during every billing circle. It has to be kept to the minimum percentage possible. The optimal use of your credit in each account per billing circle, that is a month, is 30% of your credit limit. As you make to repair your credit, be sure never to spend more than this percentage on a particular account. The implication of this is that you give the impression that you do not spend more than you can afford per cycle. To achieve this, you have to grossly cut down your expenses. If this is impossible to achieve, it is advisable to apply for multiple accounts so you can spread your expenses over the credit accounts. Your credit utilization is pivotal to your credit score. If you keep it to the barest level over the course of three to six billing cycles, you are bound to see rapid changes.

Don't Dispute without Evidence

As you continually look up your credit reports, you are bound to find errors from time to time. Sometimes, such errors are completely based on wrong pieces of information provided to the credit report bureaus. In such cases, it is justifiable to dispute such negative information. However, you should dispute with caution because excessive disputes do harm to your credit history. Over time, your disputes might not be taken seriously. You definitely do not want that for yourself. If you must dispute, ensure you do it with the required backup proofs. This leads to the next tip to bear in mind.

Keep your Credit Documents Intact

For every transaction you enter into, be sure to have enough written evidence to back it up. Such documents will come in handy if you ever have to dispute any information on your credit report. More so, never enter into any oral agreement. Keep the receipts and paperwork for all your financial commitments.

Change your Spending Habits

Attempting to repair your credit without doing away with your bad financial habits is sheer self-sabotage. You are doing yourself a long-term hurt by repairing your credit only to go back to borrowing more loans and squandering them on less important expenses. Bad habits frustrate your credit repair because you may find it difficult to meet up with your bills. If you must borrow, do so responsibly and spend it on productive matters only. Do not borrow more than you can logically refund, and do not agree to interest terms that you would find difficult to pay. Failure to pay your bills on time is one of the worst ways your creditworthiness could be hit, and, sure, you do not want debt collectors on your face all the time!

Be Careful with Credit Repair Companies

Here is an important cautionary effort. You must have been surprised at my disposition toward credit repair companies right from the onset of this book. The reasons are not farfetched. To start with, not all credit repair companies or experts are trustworthy. In a bid to garner so many clients, they make unrealistic promises and convince you that they can achieve a 720+ credit score overnight or in a few days. This is outrightly impossible. Most such companies intrude into your credit privacy, ask you for upfront payments and engage in other illegal acts but bring you little or no results. More so, you can certainly repair your credit score all by yourself.

On the overall, it is pertinent to leave you with this vital piece of advice as you embark on your credit repair: you need to stay committed to the process, give it all it requires, and that includes your efforts, time and patience. Out of desperation, you might be tempted to expect outcomes in a few days, but no, credit repair is not magic. You must be willing to give it all it takes and wait patiently for the outcome.

www.ingramcontent.com/pod-product-compliance
Lightning Source LLC
Chambersburg PA
CBHW070418220526
45466CB00004B/1451